SCHOOL
(IN)SECURITY

SCHOOL (IN)SECURITY

A COMPREHENSIVE GUIDE FOR PARENTS AND EDUCATORS
ON SCHOOL SECURITY, PROTECTING YOUR CHILDREN,
AND FOSTERING A SAFE LEARNING ENVIRONMENT

WAYNE BLACK

VIVA
EDITIONS

The opinions and recommendations expressed in this book are solely those of the author and may not be appropriate for every school. It is the responsibility of school officials and affected parents to consult with their own safety experts to determine what safety protocols would work best for their school's environment.

Published in the United States by Viva Editions, an imprint of Start Midnight, LLC, 221 River Street, Ninth Floor, Hoboken, New Jersey 07030.

Printed in the United States
Cover design: Jennifer Do
Cover image: Shutterstock
Text design: Frank Wiedemann

First Edition.
10 9 8 7 6 5 4 3 2 1

Trade paper ISBN: 978-1-63228-089-3
E-book ISBN: 978-1-63228-146-3

"We are here for the children.
Who will protect them? If not us, then who?"

—WAYNE BLACK

"Your voice is your power."

—LORI ALHADEFF, PARKLAND PARENT

TABLE OF CONTENTS

Author's Statement

The chance of more school shootings in the United States is one hundred percent. Even as we were writing this book, a six-year-old carried a handgun into Richneck Elementary School in Virginia and fired a round at their teacher without provocation. In this case, the teacher got her students to safety and survived the bullet wounds to her chest, which is nothing short of a miracle. Sadly, there will very likely be another attack on a school in this country by the time this book is published.

Will it happen at your school?

Parents, you need to stand up and be vocal about your child's security and safety at school. Teachers, it's time to be stakeholders in your own safety and the safety of the children in your care. You are the actual first responders. We will show you how to lower the chances of an active killer at your school and how to stay as safe as possible should an attack occur.

What I don't see when I visit schools, and what I do see, keeps me up at night. For me, this is a labor of love. I hope this book will save lives.

Disclaimer: Unlike most of the mass news media in this country, we will never mention the names of any killer who has attacked a school or taken the lives of our children.

This book is dedicated to all the victims of school attacks in the United States and their loved ones, past and future. Unfortunately, there will be more . . .

The following scenario is hypothetical and not based on any one incident. Some readers may find it disturbing.

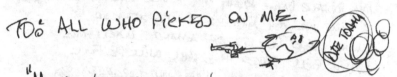

TO: ALL WHO PICKED ON ME.

"My time has FINALLY COME! I WALK through the OPEN GATE AT THE BACK OF THE FOOTBALL FIELD AND MAKE MY WAY TO ONE OF THE REAR DOORS OF THE MAIN BUILDING — which is PROPPED OPEN AS USUAL WITH A BRICK. I KNOW how to GET IN — I HAVE BEEN HERE BEFORE. I WENT TO school HERE! THE TEACHERS AND SOME OF THE STUDENTS WILL REMEMBER ME. I SURE HOPE THEY REMEMBER ME CAUSE I SURE REMBER THEM — THE ONES THAT PICKED ON ME AND MADE FUN OF ME. I 'HATE' THEM! AND I WILL SHOT THEM

THIS WILL BE A DAY that THEY WILL NEVER FORGET! I WILL BE FAMOUS FOR WHAT I DO TODAY.

THE TV NEWS WILL SHOW MY PHOTO AND TALK ABOUT ME FOR WEEKS — this is WHAT I WANT — I WANT TO SHOW THEM. THIS WILL BE JUST LIKE THE VIDEO GAME I USE TO PRACTICE WITH —

NO ONE CAN STOP ME NOW
(I AM A PUNISHER)

I WILL USE THE STAIRWELL BECAUSE THERE ARE NO CAMERAS HERE. THEN I WILL UNZIP MY DUFFLE BAG — REALLY MY RIFLE BAG ═══► AMMO
I WILL USE MY FATHER'S GUN. I ALSO HAVE 300 BULLETS OF AMMO. WHEN THE LUNCH BELL RINGS THE HALL WILL BE FULL OF STUDENTS — THEY ARE MY TARGETS ◎

MY PLANNING FOR THIS HAS TAKEN WEEKS AND I KNOW IT WILL WORK — THEY WILL BE SORRY
I AM SOOOOO READY!
I HAVE TOLD MY BEST FRIEND TO STAY HOME TODAY. I TOLD HIM WHAT I WILL DO — HE PROMISES NOT TO TELL ON ME.

THE BELL WILL RING AND I WILL HEAR MY TARGETS COMING — I WILL KEEP SHOOTING AS MANY AS I CAN — I WANT TO SET THE RECORD FOR THE MOST KILLS IN A SCHOOL!

I AM UNSTOPPABLE!

IF CLASSROOM DOORS ARE NOT LOCKED — I WILL GO THERE NEXT — LIKE THE MOVIE KILLING FIELDS — ✓
DOING IT — YEA!
THEY WILL BE SORRY!

What if I told you that this attack was being planned right now—with your child's school as the target? You don't know when, but it is going to happen with one hundred percent certainty. How would you want your school to prepare so it could either prevent the attack entirely or stop the attacker before he could get into the building?

Is what your school already doing right now to protect your children just fine? Do they keep their classroom doors locked? Are their security cameras working? Are the points of entry guarded or secure? Do you even know anything about your school's security, or do you simply trust whoever is in charge to make it a priority? Do you know who's in charge?

With school attacks on the rise in the US, it's important that you as parents become involved as real stakeholders in your child's safety. That means knowing what your school is currently doing to protect your child. Does it have a plan should the unthinkable happen?

It is far better to be prepared for the what-if than to look back days, weeks, or months after the tragedy occurs and say, "I wish I had. . . ."

INTRODUCTION

Why Are We Doing This?

When you walk into your child's school, what do you see? The bobbing heads of children moving down the hallways, teachers standing in doorways smiling as students pass, bright fluorescent lights, hand-painted posters on the walls advertising an upcoming dance or student body election. You hear the chatter and laughter and the happy commotion of the life your kids live every day when they're away from home.

When I walk into a school to do an assessment, I see something more ominous: a dark figure holding a gun standing at the end of the hallway, crouching in a stairwell, peering out from around a corner. I look at the bobbing heads of the students and the smiling faces of those teachers and ask myself: Where will they run to, what will they do, when that dark figure steps into the light . . . and fires? This is my continuing nightmare, but it is what drives me to write this book and to keep trying to convince those in charge to harden schools as potential targets.

I'm a security specialist with over forty-five years of professional security experience in both the public and private sectors. I currently own a company called Wayne Black & Associates, Inc., through which I provide threat assessments and training to schools all over the country, along with other susceptible spaces like hospitals and synagogues, churches, and other houses of worship. I also provide special firearms training for security teams and law enforcement focused on defending a school or house of worship. So, when I visit a campus or a building that houses hundreds if not thousands of young lives, my immediate instinct is to check for their security and safety. My mind just goes there; I cannot help myself.

Security professionals know that there is a one hundred percent chance of another school shooting in this country. Let me repeat that so it really sticks in your mind. There is a one hundred percent chance of more school shootings in this country. And as long as we keep saying and publishing the names of the monsters who kill our children, the copycats will keep coming out of the woodwork. Instead of making these killers the topic of the next prime-time special, we need to focus our energy on securing our schools to the point that possible attackers are dissuaded from even trying. I have a saying in regard to security: if it's predictable, it's preventable. Many of these kinds of attacks are predictable. So, why aren't they being prevented? We will explore that in detail in this book.

Active shooter, or active killer, incidents in this country and others can be traced back decades. There are countless instances throughout history where a disturbed individual has sought out innocent victims to murder. These incidents are not typical to a specific location or specific group of people. These types of mass murders have occurred in educational institutions, on military bases, at businesses, at public gatherings, and in places of worship.

In all of these incidents, many lives were affected in the wake of the destruction caused by the murder of innocent people. The other thing that has been affected and changed is law enforcement's response to such incidents. Law enforcement response plans had to change in order to keep up with the instant danger and the need to neutralize the threat as soon as possible. And there is that old saying, "When seconds count, police are minutes away."

From 1999 to 2022 in the United States of America, 169 lives were lost in mass school shootings. Most of these were children. They are not just statistics, numbers read on the news to shake your head at and hope things get better someday. They are someone's son or daughter, sister or brother, cousin, best friend, parent. Only hours before a gunman opened fire at their school, they played on playgrounds, took geometry tests, planned birthday parties, and looked forward to college or summer vacations. Their parents hugged them goodbye that morning, never in a million years thinking it would be their final goodbye.

It won't happen here, you might be thinking. *This is a safe area. Our kids go to a good school.* Maybe you even bought a house in that neighborhood because you were told it's a good school district. But what does "good" mean? Just because your school hasn't been attacked doesn't mean it won't be. In my world, this is known as a "false positive in security." Just because we have not had an incident or an attack, we think that we must be doing something right. It's a false and dangerous assumption. The parents, students, and administrations in Columbine, Sandy Hook, Parkland, and Uvalde thought the same way. They had never experienced a mass shooting at their schools . . . until they did.

It's exactly this kind of normalcy bias that lulls us into complacency, and it's this kind of complacency and denial that sometimes prevents schools from implementing the tools and the plans necessary to keep our children safe in the case of the unthinkable.

As parents, we send our children off to school to learn and to grow. We rely on the school to keep them safe and healthy. We expect, at the very least, that they will come home at the end of the day. But how do we really *know* they are safe? Who, exactly, are the people making the decisions about your child's school? Are these people actually security professionals? And how committed are they to keeping your children safe from a potential shooter or other criminal activity? And do they even know what they are doing in terms of school safety and security? Do you know the right questions to ask?

You have every right to ask these questions of your school administration and learn what is being done to keep your child safe.

It's time for parents to get fully involved before it's too late. Because just when you think *it can't happen here*, it does. Stand up now for your child! The side with the best plan wins.

What does that mean? It means that if the school's plan for security is better than the killer's plan, the school wins, and your children will be safe. However, if the potential killer's plan is better, and the school has weak security, the killer will surely succeed. Know this: in most school shootings, the active killer initially controls the environment. This is what we want to change.

Do You Know the Answers to These Questions?

It's okay to have some level of trust in your school's capability to make sound decisions for the education and safety of your children, but that doesn't mean you should not ask important questions you don't know for certain that their program is up to par.

If you didn't know what they were being taught in health class, if they were getting lunch every day, or if their math teacher was actually teaching them math, you'd be uncomfortable with that. Wouldn't you? So, it's time to step outside your comfort zone and start asking some hard questions about your child's safety:

- Who is in charge of your school's security? What is that person's background? If the answer is "our security committee," there is a problem.
- Does your school have a secure perimeter? Is there an entry gate or checkpoint, and is it enforced?
- How does your administration feel about armed police officers or armed security guards on-site?
- Are local police invited to visit the school and train at the school property after hours?
- What's your school's relationship with local emergency-response teams? When was the last meeting at the school? Do fire and police have master keys to the school?
- Do police and fire have a detailed drawing/blueprint of the school?
- What is your school's plan for an active threat?
- How much money does your school allocate to safety and security? What is the yearly budget for security? If you hear, "We don't have a budget for that this year," ask, "What is your budget for travel to conferences?"
- Does your school have a policy for reporting observable concerning behavior (OCB), also known as "red flags"?
- What is your school's policy on bullying? Is there a written policy?
- Does your school monitor/restrict student Internet activity?
- Where is your school's reunification location for parents?

- Does your school have walkie-talkies or portable radios for everyone on staff?
- Does your school have a locked-door policy for its classrooms?
- How is your school staff trained for emergency situations?
- Does your school have enough trauma kits and tourniquets on hand? How many do they have?
- Does your school health center stock Narcan?
- How are visitors to the school received and managed?

Do you know the answers to these questions? If not, it's time to ask your school administrator, principal, or headmaster. If they don't know the answers to these questions, either, or they don't want to tell you, then you likely have a safety and security problem at your school and it's time to make some immediate changes for the health and safety of your children.

Red Flags Indicating Your School May Have Security and Safety Issues

There are very few perfectly safe schools in this country. As a matter of fact, I'd posit to say there are none that are perfect, because there are always human factors involved, and those factors are so variable. But there are quite a number of schools that come close. On the other hand, there are a great many schools that have a very long way to go to protect the students and staff within their boundaries, mostly because the administration is in denial. It's time to take a critical look at your school through the lens of this list:

- If there is a "security committee" rather than a security director or full-time police officer at your school, you might have a security and safety issue.

- If there is an excuse like, "We don't have much money for security in the budget" when asked about particular aspects of security, you might have a safety issue.

- If you hear comments from school leaders like, "We don't want to live in fear" or "We want to have an open campus" or "We have never had a problem at this school," you might have a security and safety issue.

- If you hear, "Our IT department is in charge of security" or "We don't want police on campus because they may frighten students," you might have a security and safety issue.

- If you find out that the school nurse only has one tourniquet or doesn't stock Narcan, you might have a security and safety issue.

- If there are not cameras at all entrances and/or if no one is assigned to monitor the cameras at all times, you might have a security and safety issue.

- If security and ALL staff are not instantly connected by walkie-talkies at all times, you might have a security and safety issue.

- If there are no panic buttons in the main office and strategically placed around campus, you might have a security and safety issue.

- If there is no obvious climate of security in the school or among students, you might have a security and safety issue.

- If there is no clear pathway/procedure for students and parents to report observable concerning behavior, you might have a security and safety issue.

- If you have broken windows and graffiti at the school, and no action is taken to erase or repair them, you might have a school security issue.

If you don't know how your school measures up right now, it's okay. Keep reading. This book will give you a simple process to find the answers, to understand what a safe school really is, and to push for implementation of the policies and tools needed to make the eight hours a day your child spends in school the safest they can possibly be.

It's well past time for us as parents, school employees, and community members to take an active role when it comes to safety in our schools. We owe that to our children. We only get one chance to do this right.

In Loco Parentis: Who Owns Protecting Our Children?

In loco parentis literally means "in place of the parent." It refers to the type of relationship in which a person has put themselves in the situation of a parent by assuming and discharging the obligations of a parent to a child. It exists when an individual intends to take on the role of a parent, even if just for a period of time.

So, that raises a question: Is it the school's responsibility to keep our children safe in our absence? Is the safety of the students covered under in loco parentis?

According to the United States District Court in Colorado,

decision in the case of Castaldo v. Stone[1], yes, it is, and it does. The courts in this case concluded that based on their in loco parentis status, school administrators and teachers have an obligation to not only supervise students but to protect them from both physical and emotional foreseeable harm. Okay, that's cut-and-dried, right? But what is foreseeable harm? Simply put, it is potential harm that any reasonable person could predict based on the information they have, and the schools have a certain duty to know what harm could exist.

So, for example, if your school is in southern Florida, there is clearly potential for a hurricane based on the meteorological characteristics of the area. A rational person would have safety plans and tools in place for a hurricane lockdown. In Los Angeles, you'd have safety protocols in place in case of an earthquake.

In regard to school shootings, we have already said that there is a one hundred percent chance of more school attacks in the future and that these attacks may be predictable in some cases. This constitutes *foreseeable harm*, which invokes in loco parentis.

Many schools have had trespassing situations where unknown persons have been able to wander into a school building with unfettered access to classrooms and students. In these cases, we would say the school is on actual notice that security is weak.

If it is predictable, it is preventable.

It is your school's legal, ethical, and moral obligation and *duty* to implement the best possible security and safety measures to keep the children in their charge safe from harm. In some cases, like the Marjory Stoneman Douglas High School tragedy in Parkland, Florida, it was worse than foreseeable. The school, the local sheriff's office, and the FBI were all on actual notice of the

---

1   Castaldo v. Stone, 192 F. Supp. 2d 1124, 1144 (D. Colo. 2001); Doe Parents No. 1 v. Dep't of Educ., 58 P.3d 545, 585 (Haw. 2002).

potential threat from the shooter, and yet we were still left with the tragedy of seventeen lives stolen.

The following pages will equip parents and those school administrators who care about student security and safety with guidelines and concepts that will make any school a hard target. I will pass on experiences and trends that will inform parents on what to look for and what questions to ask in order to create a safe and secure school environment for their children. While we may not be able to stop all active killers at schools, if followed, these guidelines and assessment tools will surely help save lives.

Terms You Need to Know

As you read through this guidebook, it will be helpful for you to know some of the following terms, as they will pop up regularly in this book and when discussing school security in general.

Active Killer: An individual actively engaged in killing or attempting to kill people in a populated and confined area or building such as a school, church, synagogue, place of business, etc.

Active Shooter Response: Immediate response to an active killer situation, choosing an immediate and tactical course of action to neutralize the shooter(s) in order to save lives.

Breach or Probe: A testing of the waters. A perpetrator will often push a boundary or engage in some kind of misconduct to see if they'll be able to gain access to a location or weapons, or to determine if consequences will be enforced. Breaching, also called *target workup*, cannot be ignored. If a perpetrator is probing or breaching, this is a clear warning sign that they are on a trajectory toward implementing attack plans. Many times, a probe is used to determine the school's and law enforcement's response time to an attack.

Normalcy Bias/Cognitive Bias: A form of denial, cognitive or normalcy bias leads people to disbelieve or minimize threat warnings. This kind of bias or denial can seriously impede the proper implementation of security, resulting in errors that could cost lives.

Copycat Effect: Coined in 1916 after publicity over the crimes of Jack the Ripper inspired an outbreak of similar murders, this is the concept that media coverage or mass knowledge of a killer's actions will spark a series of the same type of crimes.

Drills: Practice of the school's safety protocol designed to simulate an actual emergency response. It's a common response for people to freeze in a frightening situation, but drills create a response pattern/muscle memory in our bodies and brains that will help move us in the right direction even when we are in a stressful situation. Schools should be conducting lockdown drills, evacuation drills, and reverse evacuation (taking shelter inside a building when the threat is outside) drills.

Escalation: The stages of a conflict as it worsens in response to an unresolved grievance. In threat assessment, this refers to a series of indicators prior to an incident that allow us to determine where a potential attacker lands on a trajectory toward violent attack.

Intruder: Any person who enters a private space or property without permission. A trespasser. The appropriate reaction by a school to an intruder is to activate a lockdown protocol.

Intuition: A sense of knowing something without having to focus on it. Not just a gut feeling, but a subconscious gathering of peripheral information, which is an important tool for cuing us in on our level of safety.

Lockdown: A security/safety procedure used before or during an emergency that includes immediately locking all doors, both internal and external; moving students to the central part of classrooms away from windows and doors; turning off electronic devices and silencing phones; and closing windows and blinds.

Mitigation: Reduction in the probability of a threat coming to fruition, or the capability of an institution to minimize or eliminate the casualties, fatalities, and property damage in the case of an attack or other reasonably predictable emergency.

Prevention: The actions taken to prevent an act of violence. This includes putting the proper people, tools, and plans in place to deter an attack or to stop an impending or threatening incident before it occurs.

Protection and planning: The capabilities to secure schools against acts of violence and man-made or natural disasters. Protection and planning focus on ongoing actions that protect students, teachers, staff, visitors, networks, and property from a threat or hazard.

Emergency Response Plan (ERP): The reaction of an organization to an emergency situation once it is no longer preventable and already in progress. This includes the organization's capability to mitigate or stabilize the situation; secure the safety of the people involved; prevent death, injury, and property damage; and facilitate recovery, which may include reunification in the case of a school.

Risk Factors: A condition or behavior that increases the likelihood of a particular outcome. These do not have a direct cause-and-effect relationship, but they are red flags to be aware of when it comes to factors for violence, including: antisocial behavior, illegal activity at a young age, violent role models, excessive violent video game play, bullying or being bullied, mistreatment of animals.

School Climate: The general feeling of well-being in a school, which is comprised of the relationships among students and staff, teachers, and parents, as well as with the community and the law enforcement agencies. A healthy school climate fosters respect, trust, fairness, equality, and a sense of connection among everyone involved. This is a vital element in preventing school violence.

Situational Awareness: The ability to pay attention to your surroundings, avoiding normalcy bias while noticing when something seems out of place. Understanding your environment and preattack warning signs are powerful tools in preventing acts of violence.

Targeted Violence: Premeditated attacks such as stalking, attacks on or threats against public figures, bombings, and mass attacks on schools, workplaces, places of worship, or public events. Targeted violence is aimed at a specific person, location, or group of people and is preplanned. Terrorism is targeted violence.

Threat Assessment: An information-gathering, testing process used to evaluate a school or other institution for its potential security weaknesses. This assessment may involve inspecting perimeters, communications, cameras, alarms, locks, and emergency response planning, including lockdown protocol.

Warning Signs/Observable Concerning Behavior (OCB): Also commonly known as red flags, these are actions or circumstances that point to the capability of or intention of a person to commit an act of violence. Almost all school shooters exhibited OCB prior to the attacks.

Security Operations Center (SOC): A secure location inside a school that is staffed at all times with trained professionals monitoring the school's cameras.

PART ONE:
They Thought They Were Safe

A false positive in security is when you think that just because nothing bad has happened at your school, you must be doing everything correctly. This couldn't be more wrong.

Just because nothing has happened yet doesn't mean you're safe from threats or attacks. That's like thinking you won't get your house burglarized because you haven't yet, so you leave the doors unlocked.

Whether or not your school is safe from an attack has very little to do with how "safe" your neighborhood is or whether or not it's been attacked before. As a matter of fact, if your school is not taking the proper precautions against an attack, the opposite could be true. Why?

Normalcy bias. The "it won't happen here because it hasn't yet" attitude. In my experience, many suburban and rural schools have a failure of imagination and planning when it comes to potential safety threats. They simply can't *imagine* something like that happening in a nice, quiet, safe place like this. Over the years, a failure of imagination has led to critical events being a total surprise: Pearl Harbor, the USS *Cole*, Parkland, Sandy Hook, and the September 11 attacks were all failures of imagination resulting in failures to properly plan. Our untrained minds don't always allow us to think like the enemy, so we cannot imagine such catastrophic events, thus making it close to impossible to plan.

When we fail to plan, we have planned to fail.

In heavily populated urban areas, however, the schools typically have tight security: police or security officers at entrances, metal detectors, security cameras, secured perimeters, locked doors, and an attitude of suspicion. Some of those urban schools have not become complacent because they are not limited by their inability to imagine that the worst could happen. They expect to find weapons, they expect violence, and they've prepared themselves so that the violence is hopefully stopped before it ever happens.

Unfortunately, we live in a world where normalcy bias all too often skews our thinking, especially when it comes to safety in suburban schools. How do you view your own neighborhood? Have you ever heard yourself saying things like, "It's so safe here, sometimes we even leave our doors open"? Or maybe your kids leave their bikes out in the driveway overnight, you keep your windows open to let in a cool breeze on nice afternoons, and you never feel uncomfortable taking a walk at night. You see no need for an alarm system at your home. I understand. You likely moved into that neighborhood so you *could* feel this way. But you also have to be pragmatic—just because "nothing happens here" doesn't mean it can't or won't. So, it's important to be prepared. Install that alarm system, lock your doors, and take precautions when you're walking at night. Remember the old adage: an ounce of prevention is worth a pound of cure.

It is far better to be prepared and not need it than to need it and not be prepared.

The bigger problem when it comes to normalcy biases is that they also apply to security and safety in our schools, which can lead to a very dangerous kind of complacency affecting the safety of our children.

Let's talk about the four most well-known mass killings at schools in the last quarter century: Columbine, Sandy Hook, Parkland, and Uvalde. I know you've seen them on the news, and for many of you reading this now, the Columbine massacre took place when you were in high school yourself, and it very likely shook you to your core, like it did the nation. Looking back, it's clear that normalcy bias played a part in the ability of the schools to mitigate the damage and prevent loss of life. But what did we learn from Columbine? What lessons did we take from Sandy Hook? What has changed since Parkland? And then Uvalde. . . . What will we do differently to start securing our schools against these kinds of threats?

Does your school have a real plan?

Columbine

On April 20, 1999, two senior students at Columbine High School in Columbine, Colorado, went on a forty-six-minute killing rampage after several of the ninety bombs they'd planted throughout the school and school property failed to ignite . . . and during that time, no effort was made to "engage, contain, or capture the perpetrators."[2] As a result, the attackers murdered twelve students and one teacher and injured twenty-four more students before committing suicide. Deputy fire marshal Rick Young, who disassembled the bombs, said that had the explosives detonated, the death toll would have been close to one thousand lives. The bombs were their first plan, an ode to the Oklahoma City bombing, and

---

2   Erickson, Hon. William H., *The Report of Governor Bill Owens' Columbine Review Commission* (State of Colorado, 2001).

they were planning to shoot kids as they ran out of the building after the explosion. Only by the grace of God did those bombs fail.

These two attackers had a history of bullying and being bullied, and the culture of the school seemed to turn a blind eye on bullying from jocks toward the "weaker" students. One of the attackers complained about bullying from jocks, and while both attackers were bright students, neither thrived socially. One of the attackers shifted his attention toward violent first-person-shooter video games and ran a blog about the games, wherein he became more and more graphic and "real" in his thoughts about committing heinous acts. One of his classmates' parents saw this blog, was scared because the attacker mentioned their child specifically, and reported it to the police. There was no law enforcement follow-up on the incident. The school had no plan to follow up on this troubling report, either.

Prior to the massacre at Columbine High School, both attackers were also caught breaking into a tech van to steal equipment, a crime for which they were sentenced to a diversion program where they attended classes like anger management. Both attackers submitted schoolwork depicting violence that troubled their teachers, and one even wrote a paper called "School Shooters." One attacker showed clear antiestablishment sentiment, and it's speculated that he had an undiagnosed psychotic personality disorder. There were videos, journal entries, and behaviors that should have been red flags to anyone who knew of them that went unreported and ignored.

For many of you, Columbine was the first school attack in this country during your lifetime and the largest, most devastating to that date. Some of you may have even been in high school at the time or had children in high school. In the wake of this tragedy, many Americans called for gun law reform, but a quieter cry with less media coverage was the call to drastically overhaul school security procedures in all schools nationwide. Why were those measures not taken in every school across the United States? It became clear that there was a need for more and better communication between schools and law enforcement, more and better training, more security officers on-site, tighter rules on bullying and threats, and better plans in place for catastrophic events. Yet, the sweeping reform that we might have hoped for or imagined did not actually occur.

Even right in the Commission Report on Columbine published in 2001[3], the committee denounces some of their own safety recommendations, claiming that they would be too *costly* or *impractical* for most schools to implement, and that instead, schools should make their security decisions on an as-needed basis. But that's the trouble. If you've had an issue with gang violence and weapons at school, you install metal detectors. There is a logic we can understand. However, when it comes to security against an active killer, the problem with this thought process is twofold: one, it's reactionary thinking, which is typically a day late and a dollar short; and two, with attacks like the one that occurred at Columbine, it doesn't happen until it does.

As Sandy Hook, Parkland, Uvalde, and all of the other tragic school attacks in between so clearly demonstrate, that type of thinking is a fatal mistake.

Newtown—Sandy Hook Elementary

On December 14, 2012, an armed gunman entered Sandy Hook Elementary School in Newtown, Connecticut, and took twenty-six lives before taking his own.

After shooting his mother in her home, the attacker took his

---

3   Erickson, Hon. William H., *The Report of Governor Bill Owens' Columbine Review Commission* (State of Colorado, 2001).

mother's car and all the weapons she had purchased (including the weapon he used to kill her) and drove to Sandy Hook Elementary School. He left the rifle in the car but used the AR-15 to shoot through the window next to the school's security door, where he shot and killed the principal and the school psychologist who tried to stop him. The shots were broadcast over the school's PA system, and teachers started to lock down their classrooms. The attacker entered the first classroom and killed the teacher and fourteen kids. In the second classroom, the teacher hid her students in a closet and told him that her class was in the auditorium. He shot and killed the teacher and six children who ran out of the closet.

At this point, police had been called and arrived on-site just as the attacker turned his Glock 20 ten-millimeter pistol on himself. They found him dead, along with a total of twenty elementary school students and six teachers and staff members.

Unlike the Columbine killers, the attacker at Sandy Hook did not openly express his intention to commit an act of violence. There were no real indicators, even to the attacker's former therapists. However, according to the official Report of the Ansonia-Milford Judicial District State's Attorney[4], the attacker had recently scouted the area, and investigators uncovered some disturbing evidence in the attacker's home, including a number of violent video games such as *Left for Dead*, *Metal Gear Solid*, *Dead Rising*, *Half Life*, *Battlefield*, *Call of Duty*, *Grand Theft Auto*, *Shin Megami Tensei*, *Dynasty Warriors*, *Vice City*, *Team Fortress*, and *Doom*. He also had in his possession the following items, as listed in the official report[4]: a Christmas check from the mother to the shooter to purchase a CZ 83 firearm; a *New*

---

4   Sedensky, Stephen J. III, *Report of the State's Attorney for the Judicial District of Danbury on the Shootings at Sandy Hook Elementary School 36 Yogananda Street, Newtown Connecticut on December 14, 2012* (State of Connecticut, 2013). https://portal.ct.gov/-/media/DCJ/SandyHookFinalReportpdf.pdf

York Times article from February 18, 2008, regarding the school shooting at Northern Illinois University; three photographs of what appear to be a dead human, covered in blood and wrapped in plastic; the book *Amish Grace: How Forgiveness Transcended Tragedy*, Jossey-Bass, 2007, by Donald B. Kraybill, Steven Nolt, and David Weaver-Zercher; and photocopied newspaper articles from 1891 pertaining to the shooting of schoolchildren.

In addition, the investigation uncovered the following electronic evidence taken from the attacker's computer, also listed in the report:

- Bookmarks pertaining to firearms, military, politics, mass murder, video games, music, books, Army Rangers, computers and programs, ammunition, candy, and economics books
- Webpage design folders
- Two videos showing suicide by gunshot
- Commercial movies depicting mass shootings
- A computer game titled *School Shooting*, where the player controls a character who enters a school and shoots at students
- Screen shots (172) of the online game *Combat Arms*
- *Dance Dance Revolution* (DDR) game screen shots
- Videos of shooter playing *DDR*
- Images of the shooter holding a handgun to his head
- Images of the shooter holding a rifle to his head
- Five-second video (dramatization) depicting children being shot
- Images of shooter with a rifle, shotgun, and numerous magazines in his pockets

- Documents on weapons and magazine capacity
- A document written showing the prerequisites for a mass murder spreadsheet
- A spreadsheet listing mass murders by name and information about the incident
- Materials regarding the topic of pedophilia and advocating for rights for pedophiles (not child pornography)
- Large number of materials relating to Columbine shootings and documents on mass murders
- Large number of materials on firearms

From this evidence it's clear to me that the attacker was preoccupied with killing, with children, and was intrigued by the Columbine killing, the massacres that took place at the Amish schoolhouse called West Nickel Mines school in 2006, and the shooting at Northern Illinois University in 2008, indicating that the copycat effect was a factor in his actions at Sandy Hook Elementary School.

In this situation, the attacker didn't openly demonstrate any observable behavior. It was all buried on the Internet (not in chat rooms, where other people could see it) or in his private living space. Additionally, the actions of the school faculty and police were appropriate. The tools that could have potentially saved lives in this situation would have been barriers to entry onto school property, armed security at the door, and locked classroom doors. The entire incident, from killing his grandmother to the last gunshot, lasted less than two hours and took twenty-seven lives.

Parkland—Marjory Stoneman Douglas High School

On February 14, 2018, fourteen students and three staff members were killed by a gunman at Marjory Stoneman Douglas High School in Parkland, Florida. Another seventeen were injured. The horrible attack left the community shocked and devastated. We are going to spend a little more time going through this incident, as well as the Uvalde attack, in greater detail so that we can more specifically point out the times that this travesty could have been prevented and the tools that could have been utilized to stop this killer before he inflicted so much harm.

The following information about the attack on MSD was gathered from the official MSD Public Safety Commission Report issued on January 2, 2019[5].

At 2:19 p.m., the attacker was dropped off by a ride-share service. He was carrying a duffel bag and wearing a MSD T-shirt. He entered through an open gate and was seen by a campus monitor. At 2:21:16 he entered the building through an unlocked door and quickly ducked into the stairwell, where he put on a magazine-carrying vest and loaded his semiautomatic rifle. While he was loading his rifle, a student stepped into the stairwell, and the attacker told her she better get out of there, that something bad was about to happen. The student fled the building. At 2:21:33, the attacker stepped out of the stairwell, lifted his rifle, checked it, then lifted it again. At that point, he fired, killing three students (Martin Duque, Luke Hoyer, and Gina Montalto) and injuring a fourth (Ashley Baez). Everything happened so fast at this point that most students didn't even have time to react.

Then at 2:21:40, the attacker turned his rifle to room 1216 and

---

5   Marjory Stoneman Douglas Public Safety Commission, *Initial Report Submitted to the Governor, Speaker of the House of Representatives and Senate President* (State of Florida, 2019). http://www.fdle.state.fl.us/MSDHS/CommissionReport.pdf

opened fire, fatally shooting Alyssa Alhadeff, Alaina Petty, and Alex Schachter, and injuring William Olson, Genesis Valentin, Justin Colton, Alexander Dworet, and Kheshava Managapuram. Just two minutes and forty seconds after he stepped out of his ride-share, six young people had been killed and five injured. But it did not stop there. Not yet. Ashley Baez ran from the alcove of the women's restroom into a classroom, and he shot her in the thigh. At this point, the attacker dropped to a knee and removed some camouflage clothing from his bag, along with a ski mask, but he left them on the floor and lifted his rifle again. He fired into classroom 1214, killing Nicholas Dworet and Helena Ramsay and injuring Isabel Chequer, Samantha Fuentes, Samantha Grady, and Daniela Menescal.

At this same time, Coral Springs Communication Center received a 911 call from inside Building 12. At 2:22:14, Deputy Scot Peterson met Security Specialist Kelvin Greenleaf in front of Building 1. Fire alarms were going off in Building 12 and several other buildings on campus. Students in Room 1255 on the third floor screamed as twenty students from classroom 1250 ran down the hallway in panic. The attacker fired into classroom 1216 again, and several students on the second floor also ran, panicked, into classrooms to hide.

At 2:22:48, Campus Monitor Chris Hixon entered the first-floor hallway from the west end and ran east. The attacker turned west from where he was standing in front of rooms 1216 and 1217 and shot Hixon, who instantly fell to the ground. While the attacker paused in front of rooms 1214 and 1215, Hixon managed to crawl across the floor and hide behind a wall. At this time, the group of twenty kids that had run from room 1250 turned back around in the stairwell, most likely hearing the shots fired. That's where they ran into a number of students calmly exiting as if it were just an ordinary fire drill. However, on the second floor, all students were already locked down in their classrooms and the hallways were empty. No students were shot on the second floor.

In Building 12, all shots were fired from the hallway either toward people running in the hallway or through classroom doors or windows.

At 2:22:57, the fire alarms were shut off. At 2:23:05, the attacker stepped into the alcove for classrooms 1212 and 1213. He fired, killing Carmen Schentrup and injuring Samantha Mayor, Madeleine Wilford, and Ben Wikander. Meanwhile, the third-floor hallway was filled with students casually exiting like a typical fire drill. In fact, one hundred students filled the east end of the third-floor hallways as the attacker started to move again. They had no clue that there was an active shooter in the building. No code red had been called.

At 2:23:14, the attacker walked west on the first floor, passing by Chris Hixon and shooting him again. At 2:23:17, Deputy Peterson arrived at the east side of the building, being joined seconds later by Security Specialist Greenleaf and Campus Monitor Andrew Medina. Students hesitated at the top of the east stairwell.

Back on the first floor, Campus Monitor Aaron Feis stepped into the west stairwell from the exterior at the same time the attacker stepped into the stairwell from the interior. The attacker shot and killed Coach Feis and continued up the west stairwell toward the second floor. At 2:23:26, Deputy Peterson radioed about "possible shots fired." A mass of students moved shoulder to shoulder at the east end of the third floor and crowded around the stairs, some actually making their way down the stairs. At 2:23:30, teacher Ernest Rospierski redirected a group of those students casually walking to the west stairwell, pushing them toward the east. Two seconds later, the attacker raised his rifle on the west end of the second floor, but the hallway was deserted. He didn't fire at that time but would later return to fire six rounds on the second floor, none of which hit anyone. He moved east, making statements like "no one is here" as he walked down the hall. Meanwhile, the third floor was jammed with students who were mostly clueless or confused about the severity of what was happening just below them.

The second-floor students treated the situation as an active killer response, so they were hiding in their classrooms. When the attacker couldn't immediately see them through the windows, he refrained from shooting. He kept moving east down the hallway. At this point, Deputy Peterson and Security Specialist Greenleaf had retreated to the stairs on the northeast corner of Building 7. Deputy Peterson would be in this location for the next forty-eight minutes.

On the third floor, Rospierski heard rounds fired into the second-floor classroom 1231 and instantly reacted, ushering panicking students into classrooms. Unfortunately, his own classroom door had locked behind them when they left, so he also spent time looking for his keys to open it up and get kids in. Other third floor teachers also stood holding their doors open to get kids in. The stairwells emptied and most of the students on the ends of the hallway relocated, but a crowd still remained in the middle of the third-floor hall. The attacker fired into second-floor classroom 1234, hitting an exterior classroom window located about seventy feet from where Deputy Peterson was located.

At 2:24:32, the attacker fired on the group in the third-floor hallway, killing teacher Scott Beigel along with students Jaime Guttenberg, Cara Loughran, Joaquin Oliver, Meadow Pollack, and Peter Wang, and injuring Anthony Borges, Marian Kabachenko, Kyle Laman, and teacher Stacey Lippel.

Rospierski ducked into his classroom's alcove with about nine students. Joaquin Oliver and Meadow Pollack ran into the women's restroom alcove, while Kyle Laman ran into the men's restroom alcove. But the women's restroom was locked, so Pollack ran to Rospierski's classroom alcove, which was getting very full. Oliver tried the men's restroom, which was also locked. Apparently there had been an issue with students vaping in these classrooms, resulting in those doors being locked.

At 2:24:45, Rospierski had tried the door of the neighboring classroom, but it was also locked. At 2:24:50, the attacker put a new magazine in his rifle and began walking west in the hallway. Rospierski and ten students fled toward the west stairwell. Pollack was shot, and Loughran stayed in the alcove.

At 2:24:54, the first verifiable code red was called by Campus Monitor Elliott after he found Feis's body outside Building 12. Four seconds later, the attacker fired at the students fleeing toward the stairwell. Eight of them made it, but Rospierski stayed on the landing with Guttenberg and Wang, who had been shot. The attacker then shot Pollack and Loughran, who remained in the classroom alcove, and Oliver, who was hiding in the restroom alcove.

He continued to fire rounds until he approached the stairwell door, behind which Rospierski was concealed, but he wasn't able to open it, so he moved on to the teachers' lounge, where he attempted to set up a sniper position. At 2:26:54, CSPD Officer T. Burton arrived on campus and radioed his arrival. There were eight BSO deputies on or around the campus from 2:27:03 to 2:27:10, and all of them reported hearing the attacker's last gunshots, but none of them entered the building to look for the shooter.

Fifteen seconds after he fired his last shot, the attacker ditched his vest and 180 live rounds in the west stairwell and fled the building using the west exit. He ran between Buildings 6 and 13, then switched south by Building 9 and tailed a group of students also fleeing the buildings. At this point, deputies on-site were told by Deputy Peterson to stay five hundred feet away from Building 12, and a radio transmission went out at 2:29:16 from Officer Burton saying the attacker was ". . . last seen in the three-story building, north parking lot."[5] At 2:29:35 Lieutenant Mike DeVita and Captain Jan Jordan went into the administration building, while seconds later the attacker blended into a large group of students fleeing toward Westglades Middle School.

At 2:32:42, more than five minutes after deputies heard the last of the attacker's shots fired, four CSPD officers entered Building 12 using the west entry while BSO deputies were stationed outside the door. At 2:37:18, Captain Jordan met BSO Sergeant Ian Sklar in Building 8's parking lot, where Captain Jordan discovered that neither of his radios worked properly. They then moved to Holmberg Road, near the west parking lot entrance, and at 2:40:16, the first mass student evacuation began.

Almost eight minutes later, law enforcement had searched the office and all of the first-floor classrooms while Sergeant Richard Rossman spoke with Assistant Principal Winfred Porter and Campus Monitor Medina about the school camera system and anything they'd seen during the attack. Meanwhile, the attacker walked through a nearby Walmart parking lot, then into the Subway inside the Walmart, and got a drink. Back at the high school, BSO Sergeant Rossman and CSPD Officer Richard Best radioed that the attacker was last seen on the second floor, and about two minutes later, BSO-SWAT Sergeant Anthony Garcia and a group of officers entered the second-floor landing of Building 12, believing the attacker to still be inside the building.

The attacker left Walmart at 2:53:40, and less than a minute later, BSO Sergeant Rossman radioed that the attacker had moved from the third floor to the second floor, which was then also broadcast by CSPD Captain Brad Mock. Then Rossman was notified by the assistant principal that the camera information wasn't a livestream, but it took him another seven minutes to broadcast that over BSO radio. BSO-SWAT Captain Steve Robson met Captain Jordan north of Building 13 at 2:59:59 and 23 seconds later, CSPD Captain Ryan Gallagher radioed the CSPD channel that the video wasn't in real time; it was on a delay.

The attacker walked into a nearby McDonald's at 3:01:03 and sat down at a table with another MSD student named John Wilford. Neither of them realized it at the time, but the attacker had just shot and wounded Wilford's sister, Madeleine. A little over a minute later, the attacker walked south out of the McDonald's. It was at about this time that it was broadcast over BSO radio by Sergeant Rossman that the surveillance video was on a delay and that the attacker had "fled Building 12 approximately twenty minutes earlier."[6]

At 3:03:00, responders had removed fifteen victims from the first floor of Building 12, two of whom died from their injuries. The second-floor classrooms were checked and cleared by 3:03:22, and at 3:07:15, Anthony Borges, the last surviving victim, was brought out by law enforcement and SWAT medics. By 3:09:40, law enforcement had checked all doors and gained control of the stairwells and hallways of Building 12. Almost two minutes later, Deputy Peterson left his position at Building 7, where he had stayed for the duration of the incident—approximately forty-eight minutes. At 3:16:44, BSO Colonel James Polan arrived at the Tactical Operations Center (TOC) located in the student parking lot north of Building 13 and took over as incident commander.

At 3:17:53, the BSO Mobile Command Center arrived on Pine Island Road near campus and Captain Mock radioed that he was

---

6   Marjory Stoneman Douglas Public Safety Commission, *Initial Report Submitted to the Governor, Speaker of the House of Representatives and Senate President* (State of Florida, 2019). http://www.fdle.state.fl.us/MSDHS/CommissionReport.pdf

with BSO and their command staff, marking the first verified direct communication between BSO incident commander(s) and CSPD command staff.

Finally, at about 3:37:45, Officer Michael Leonard of the Coconut Creek Police Department detained the attacker approximately two miles from the Marjory Stoneman Douglas High School campus.

Unlike the perpetrators of the attacks on Columbine and Sandy Hook, this attacker thought he could get away with it. He didn't take his own life like the previous three killers had. Instead, he fled. So, why did he do it? Were there any observable concerning behaviors surrounding this attacker prior to the shooting?

In fact, there were many.

The attacker was adopted at birth, but his adoptive father died of a heart attack in 2004, and three months prior to the Parkland massacre, his mother also died, leaving him orphaned and living with various family members. He was a troubled child and had suffered from mental health and behavioral issues since he was very young. He was moved from school to school and finally, in 2014, into a school in the district specifically for students with emotional or learning disabilities. There, he fared better than he had in traditional schools, but he still demonstrated disruptive and combative behavior.

He was diagnosed with a number of mental health disabilities including depression, autism, ADHD, and a behavior disorder, and as early as 2013, it was recommended by mental health professionals that he be put into a residential treatment facility.[7] He had a number of visits from counselors and Child and Family Services throughout the years due to either altercations or instances where

---

7 Marjory Stoneman Douglas Public Safety Commission, *Initial Report Submitted to the Governor, Speaker of the House of Representatives and Senate President* (State of Florida, 2019). http://www.fdle.state.fl.us/MSDHS/CommissionReport.pdf

he said he was suicidal, none of which resulted in mandated hospitalization for observation.

In 2016, he moved to Marjory Stoneman Douglas High, where he participated in junior ROTC but was eventually banned from shooting guns during practice due to some disturbing behavior. Around this same time, a former middle school friend ran into him at a dollar store where he worked. During their brief interaction, the attacker told the former friend that he hated MSD and was going to shoot it up. He played it off as an "I'm kidding" statement, but the comment stuck with that friend. Unfortunately, it was not reported to the school or law enforcement.

Also in 2016, the attacker was prohibited from carrying a backpack into the school due to the school's concern over his disturbing fascination with guns.

When the attacker turned eighteen, a social worker who had had contact with him filed a report expressing MSD's concern about the attacker's desire to purchase a gun, and she noted that the school would be implementing a safety plan. Also at this time, a teacher expressed concern over the attacker's having written the word *Kill* in a notebook. He was apparently angry with his mother for not taking him to get the state ID that would be required for gun purchase.

On February 8, 2017, he was transferred to an alternative school due to his repeated behavioral issues. Three days later, he visited a gun store and purchased the AR-15 that he would use a year later to attack Marjory Stoneman Douglas High. During that year, his mother died, and he moved in with a neighbor. On November 28, 2017, shortly after his mother's passing, a 911 operator received a call from that neighbor saying that the attacker was violent, punching holes in walls and demanding that she give him his gun and the bullets she was keeping away from him.

This is a person who slipped through the cracks on numerous

occasions throughout his life, and especially leading up to the attack on February 14, 2018. At that point, the opportunity to report and act on the red flags was over.

So much went wrong at Marjory Stoneman Douglas before and during the horrific attack. Observable concerning behavior went unaddressed or not addressed in the most appropriate manner, and warning signs were ignored. Once the attacker was at the school, he entered through an open, unguarded gate, walked right through an unlocked door, and shot into unlocked classrooms. The students and teachers were not properly coached on how to react in an active killer situation. There was a failure of leadership and a failure of communication on the part of school resource officers and law enforcement agencies. The list is extensive, and what could have been prevented turned into a horrible tragedy.

Uvalde—Robb Elementary School

While I'm sure most of you have seen the videos on the news, read the articles, and heard the story of one of the most recent high-fatality school attacks in the United States, you may not know the details in their entirety. Not unlike MSD in Parkland, the killings in Uvalde were the direct result of a series of utter failures by school administrators, school police, and local law enforcement. The following is a brief recap of the tragic incident that occurred in the small Texas town of Uvalde, summarized from the official report published on July 17, 2022, by the Texas House of Representatives Investigative Committee on the Robb Elementary School Shooting[8]:

---

8   Rep. Dustin Burrows, Rep. Joe Moody and Honorable Eva Guzman, *Texas House of Representatives Investigative Committee on the Robb Elementary Shooting* (State of Texas, 2022). https://www.documentcloud.org/documents/22088422-robb-elementary-investigative-committee-report-fullsize

At 11:35 a.m. that day, according to the Texas Department of Public Safety, the officers who responded to the call and were stationed outside the school were shot at by a gunman, suffering "grazing wounds." (I am not sure that the "grazing wounds" didn't come from other officers, but this is what's been officially reported.) Instead of pursuing the gunman to prevent him from entering the school, the officers *retreated*. When the Uvalde school police chief arrived on-site at some point later, he did not have a police radio with him. He had no way to effectively communicate a strategy to other officers, no way to take control of the situation. Nationally, the law enforcement plan for active killers is that the first officer on the scene is to push forward and engage the active killer(s), to neutralize the threat. In this case, at least one police officer observed the shooter entering the school with a rifle. The officer hesitated and did not engage. Rather, he actually asked on the radio for permission to shoot the active killer instead of engaging, which I believe would have ended the event immediately.

But hold on, let's backtrack just a little bit here. This is the sound bite that a lot of us will hear or read, but there are a lot of details missing from that summation and a lot of backstory that bears importance to the outcome. There were observable concerning behaviors, warning signs, as far back as two months prior to the event and as close to the event as that very morning. If they had been reported and dealt with properly, the observation of these behaviors and action steps to intervene either with heightened security or with mental health care could possibly have prevented this tragedy.

First, we need to dig into the attacker's personal history. He was eighteen years old at the time of the attack. Up until that point, he had a minimal relationship with his father and a troubled relationship with his single mother, who reportedly had a history of drug abuse. At the time of the attack, the attacker lived with his grandmother very close to Robb Elementary School. He had had trouble in school since he was very young: bullying, low grades, spotty school attendance, and possibly an unaddressed learning disability, combined with severe poverty, which caused him to occasionally wear the same clothing for multiple days in a row, which only encouraged the social ostracizing.

He struggled with self-esteem all the way into his teen years, resulting in an eating disorder and other self-destructive behaviors including withdrawing socially and turning to violent video games, online chat rooms, and violent pornography. Again, via online chat rooms, he talked often about gore, violent sex, and suicide and presented himself (according to other people who had contact with him via this avenue) as detached, inhuman, and a sociopath. This paints a picture of a person who is an outsider, feeling misunderstood and perhaps abandoned, and even likely with an undiagnosed and untreated mental illness. Ultimately, he had a horrible fight with his mother and moved in with his grandmother near Robb Elementary School, where he slept on the floor of the living room. He was a social outcast with violent tendencies. This is a person who should have had an eye kept on him.

Now that you have a picture of what this attacker's state of mind may have been like when he made the decision to move forward with his plans, let's look at the series of actual events leading up to the attack on Robb Elementary School on May 24, 2022.

According to the report, the following is a general timeline of some clear, observable concerning behaviors surrounding the attacker, none of which were reported to the school, the police department, or any other organization or person in a position to investigate further:

- Late 2021: The attacker posted a video of himself holding a clear plastic bag containing a dead cat shortly after posting remarks indicating he was jealous of a person who abused animals and was made famous by a Netflix documentary. (Sound familiar? Same as the Parkland shooter.)
- Late 2021: The attacker is fired from his fast food job after repeatedly threatening a female coworker.
- Late 2021: The attacker purchased shin guards, rifle slings, a red dot sight, and body armor and asked at least two people to purchase guns for him (as he was only seventeen), of which his family was aware.
- Late 2021: He earned the nickname "Yubo's School Shooter" on the Yubo platform because of his obsession with school shootings and the posts of himself wearing body armor and holding a BB gun. The nickname "school shooter" was also adopted on other social media platforms and was commonly used, but his behavior or remarks were never reported.
- Early 2022: The attacker had a violent argument with his mother, which was livestreamed on Instagram, after which he moved in with his grandma. This could be considered an inciting incident, because it is at this point that he began to put his plans into action.
- Early 2022: The attacker's father noticed self-inflicted cuts on his son's face, and the boy reportedly said that he was "going to do something soon."

- February 2022: The attacker ". . . began buying more firearms accessories beginning in February 2022, including 60 30-round magazines, a holographic weapon sight, and a Hellfire Gen 2 Snap-On trigger system."
- May 16, 2022: The attacker turned eighteen, and on that very day he:
  - Purchased 1,740 rounds of 5.56-millimeter 75-grain boat tail hollow-point bullets—$1,761.50
  - Ordered a Daniel Defense DDM4 V7 (an AR-15–style rifle) to be shipped to a Uvalde gun store—$2,054.28
- May 17, 2022: At the same Uvalde gun store, the attacker purchased another AR-15–style rifle, a Smith and Wesson M&P15—$1,081.42
- May 18, 2022: The attacker returned to the same gun store and purchased 375 rounds of M193 ammunition.
- May 20, 2022: The attacker picked up his ordered rifle and had the staff install the holographic sight.

The report indicates that in interviews with the investigative team, the gun store owner didn't see any red flags and only asked how such a young kid could afford all of this. However, in later interviews with gun store patrons, they claimed the attacker appeared to be nervous and gave off "bad vibes." However, the background check was completed, and he was cleared for legal purchase. Unfortunately, "While multiple gun sales within such a short period are and were reported to the ATF [Department of Alcohol, Tobacco, and Firearms], the law only requires purchases of handguns to be reported to the local sheriff. Here, the information about the attacker's gun purchases remained in federal hands."[9]

Also, since the attacker did not have a driver's license and did not drive, his uncle drove him twice either to or from the location (once under false pretenses) and allowed the gun to be stored at his home, since his grandmother wouldn't allow guns in her house. He also witnessed the attacker attempting to seat a magazine in the rifle.

May 23, 2022: A suspicious, dark-clothed figure with a backpack was seen casing the school. The figure was never identified. At that time, security should have been heightened as a result, but that is not indicated.

May 23, 2022, evening: The attacker sent out numerous vague messages that alluded to his plans to attack a school, including a Snapchat message to a German friend that said he had a plan that he wouldn't be able to carry out until his package arrived later that evening.

May 24, 2022, morning: The attacker FaceTimed the same German friend while having an argument with his grandma. After hanging up, he texted her,

"I just shot my grandma in the head"

"Ima go shoot up an elementary school rn"

Her response, which she deleted prior to sending the screenshot of their conversation to authorities after hearing about the shooting on the news, was: "Cool."

This is where the opportunity to report the observable concerning behavior and follow up on the red flags ends.

---

9   Rep. Dustin Burrows, Rep. Joe Moody and Honorable Eva Guzman, *Texas House of Representatives Investigative Committee on the Robb Elementary Shooting* (State of Texas, 2022). https://www.documentcloud.org/documents/22088422-robb-elementary-investigative-committee-report-fullsize

On May 24, at 11:28 a.m., the attacker crashed his grand-mother's truck into a drainage ditch in front of Hillcrest Memorial Funeral Home right next door to Robb Elementary. Two men ran out from the funeral home to check on the wreck, and the attacker fired shots at them. They retreated and called 911, telling the dispatcher that he was headed toward the school. The attacker proceeded to throw his backpack over the five-foot-tall fence and jump over into the schoolyard.

Coach Yvette Silva was on the playground with a group of third graders. She saw the attacker, who was firing shots toward them, and immediately put her group of kids into lockdown mode, using her school radio to convey this message: "Coach Silva to office, somebody just jumped over the fence and he's shooting."[3] Unfortunately, she did not immediately hear a lockdown directive called. Principal Mandy Gutierrez was in her office when she received the call, and she initiated lockdown over the Raptor app, but poor Internet connectivity interrupted the alert. She did not call a lockdown over the intercom but instead called Sergeant Arredondo and told the custodian, Jaime Perez, to make sure all the doors were locked. Perez had already heard Silva's radio call and had begun locking doors from the inside.

The question here is "Why weren't the doors already locked?"

In the meantime, Uvalde Police Sergeant Eduardo Canales, commander of the SWAT team, and Lieutenant Mariano Pargas, the acting chief of the Uvalde Police, went to the funeral home and then entered school grounds, where they met Lieutenant Javier Martinez. Sergeant Daniel Coronado then arrived, meeting two other police officers who said that based on the echo, they believed the shooter was firing at them. None of them had their eyes on the attacker, so they could not confirm his location. One of those officers asked Sergeant Coronado for permission to shoot at a black-clothed adult running away from them toward the group of children also running away on the playground, believing this to be the shooter. Before Coronado could respond, they heard the report that the shooter was moving toward the school. The black-clothed person running in the playground was Robb Elementary coach Abraham Gonzales.

Moments later, Chief Arredondo arrived from his office at Uvalde High School after hearing reports of gunshots fired. However, his radios were cumbersome, so he left them at the fence with an understanding that Sergeant Coronado would be fully uniformed with his radio. Meanwhile, teachers began to hear that there was an armed man on campus and began to initiate a lockdown response as the attacker walked west along the wall of the west building and entered through the unlocked door. Two other exterior doors of that building were also unlocked. He made his way east inside the building.

At 11:33 a.m., he fired into adjoined classrooms 111 and 112, entering through classroom 111, as it had been previously reported to have a faulty lock and did not secure properly. The attacker spent two and a half minutes in those classrooms, firing one hundred rounds. Law enforcement officers just arriving on campus, as well as frightened teachers and students, heard this blast of gunfire. At the same time, approximately 11:36 a.m., Uvalde Police Department dispatch received a call reporting a woman "shot in the head on Diaz Street."[10]

Responders entered the building through the south and west doors, and over the next five minutes from the time of their entry, the attacker fired sixteen more rounds. The officers claim that while they heard the hundred-round burst of gunfire, they did

---

10 Rep. Dustin Burrows, Rep. Joe Moody and Honorable Eva Guzman, *Texas House of Representatives Investigative Committee on the Robb Elementary Shooting* (State of Texas, 2022). https://www.documentcloud.org/documents/22088422-robb-elementary-investigative-committee-report-fullsize

not hear screams or any indication that victims had been shot inside the classrooms and so did not respond to aid them. When law enforcement officers reached rooms 111 and 112, they noticed what appeared to be smoke in the rooms and shell casings on the ground, and then the attacker fired at them from inside the room and they were hit with fragments. They retreated down the hallway or exited the building. Other officers arrived and remained at the end of the hallway. Meanwhile, another group of officers moved in from the south side, but they were having trouble communicating via radio.

Chief Arredondo then saw a light on in room 110, entered, and determined it was empty. He hoped the same was true about 111 and 112, and at that point Arredondo determined this was no longer an active shooter scenario, but a "barricaded subject" scenario, wherein their priority switched to protecting the people in the other classrooms. Responders claim that they had no visual confirmation that there were people inside the rooms inhabited by the shooter and concluded that it was a bailout situation. This course of action never changed, even when Chief Arredondo concluded at some point during that next forty-seven minutes that there must be injuries and/or fatalities in those two rooms. This proved to be a tragic mistake.

At this point, Arredondo checked room 109 and saw children inside. Gonzalez asked the chief if he wanted to activate the SWAT team (which was already in the building), and he answered in the affirmative. Then, Arredondo phoned the Uvalde Police Department to ask for supplies and backup. At 11:42 a.m., Constable Johnny Field arrived and communicated with Arredondo via cell phone. They agreed to begin evacuating students, and officers began breaking windows to do this. Sergeant Coronado made his own report, asking for helicopter support and ballistic shields. At this time, he told dispatch that the attacker was barricaded in the room and that he did not know if the door was locked and requested mirrors to check the classroom for students. He remained outside the building for the next thirty minutes, helping with evacuation efforts and advising arriving responders to be aware of potential crossfire in the hallway. When it was suggested to him that he clear the hallway because a United States Border Patrol Tactical Unit (BORTAC) was moving in, his response was that Arredondo was there and in charge of the operation.

Arredondo spent much of the next forty minutes searching for a master key and trying to get breaching tools to get into the classroom while communicating with the attacker in both English and Spanish. However, he was not made aware when such tools arrived on-site. Furthermore, nobody ever contacted the principal or custodian, both of whom had master keys. Four more shots were fired inside the classrooms at 12:21 p.m. At 12:30 p.m., more officers stacked the hallways outside the classroom as they waited for BORTAC to initiate its breach. At 12:45 p.m., a set of keys was located, and at 12:50 p.m., BORTAC officers breached the classroom and killed the attacker. One officer was injured in this effort. Officer Arredondo testified that he did not make the decision for BORTAC to breach the classroom, stating that he only directed officers to test the keys and evacuate classrooms.

To backtrack a little bit, after Lieutenant Martinez recovered from the initial shock of that first gunfire where he and his fellow officer were hit with fragments, he turned back toward classrooms 111 and 112 in an effort to advance (as his active shooter training dictated), but no other officers followed to back him up, an example of the cowardly response of the Uvalde police force. Officers testified to the counsel that, had Lieutenant Martinez had backup at that point, he might have made it to the classrooms and engaged. Instead, he retreated to help in the effort to evacuate children and then returned to the hallway as part of the stack of officers to back up BORTAC when they initiated their breaching effort.

From 11:37 a.m. when Martinez, Canales, and Louis Landry made their first retreat, until 12:50 p.m., when BORTAC breached the classroom, dozens of law enforcements officers were in and out of that north hallway preparing to assist in the breach effort. The Uvalde Police Department set up a control office at the funeral home next door but did not succeed in commanding the operation, claiming that Chief Arredondo had jurisdiction and must be coordinating the effort from inside. But sadly, Chief Arredondo did not successfully take any kind of command, and despite the fact that the Uvalde Police were receiving 911 calls from inside the building claiming gunshot injuries, the direction of the effort did not switch to "active shooter" from "barricaded suspect," nor did any first responders attempt to get to the victims to aid them until way too late. One officer, Special Agent Luke Williams, ignored orders to secure the perimeter and instead entered the building and began to evacuate students.

Sometime between 11:52 a.m. and 12:21 p.m., four ballistic shields arrived at the north side of the building, but only one was protective against rifles like the AR-15 being used by the attacker. Even so, Chief Arredondo, on the other side of the building, was not made aware of the arrival of any shields at all. At 12:30 p.m., there was a flurry of activity: officers began to enter the building to stack the hallways, medical triage equipment was set up at the east side of the north hallway, and the arrival of BORTAC was announced—it is obvious that when BORTAC arrived, it quickly took command of the situation.

Commander Paul Guerrero, assisted by a BORTAC team and covered with the ballistic shield, unlocked the door (which was likely already unlocked due to a faulty locking mechanism), and entered the room. The attacker fired at the officers from the corner of the room, but they also fired, killing the active shooter.

Failure to take command prevented law enforcement officers from enacting an effective plan to mitigate this attack. Witnesses at the scene described it as "chaos." Most responders assumed that Chief Arredondo was taking command, but that was clearly not happening, especially without any radio contact. Starting at 12:03 p.m., there was a series of communications with a student inside room 112, making it very clear that there were students inside and there were injuries, and yet Arredondo never switched the response from a barricaded suspect to an active shooter response. He was not coordinating efforts between the various law enforcement agencies that arrived on-site, nor was he even in consistent communication with the officers he knew were on the south side of the building. Later, Chief Arredondo claimed that he believed the Uvalde Police Department held command upon their arrival, but there was nothing to indicate this was the case.

All in all, 376 responders from twenty-three different agencies arrived on-site at Robb Elementary School on May 24, 2022, with no one clearly in command until BORTAC arrived, when Commander Guerrero quickly took charge, bringing the situation to an end after a deadly hour and twenty-two minutes.

This report leaves me with so many questions, as it should you, such as:

Why were the attacker's observable concerning behaviors not reported?
There are a number of reasons that people do not report red flags like the attacker demonstrated in Uvalde. One is that, oftentimes, someone will think that someone else is going to report it, so they shouldn't concern themselves over it. It's not their responsibility.

Another reason is that people do not know how or where to report these behaviors. A third possibility is that they simply don't take these red flags seriously.

Why were the door-locking policies blatantly ignored in some cases, and in other cases, broken locking mechanisms left in disrepair?
Normalcy bias plays a role here: "It's safe here, we've never had a problem, and it's inconvenient to keep the doors locked." School police didn't have a plan with school administrators to check doors to make sure all locks worked and were being used.

Why didn't the Uvalde Police Department call the school and tell them to initiate lockdown as soon as they received the 911 call from the funeral home?
Failure to build a concrete relationship between the first responder agencies and the school, and to establish a clear protocol, is a potentially fatal but all too common mistake.

Why didn't the officers "push" until the shooter was barricaded, surrendered, or neutralized? Why did they wait in the hallway for forty-five minutes?
Groupthink plays a role in this. The officers hung back and waited because one hung back. Then, when their commanding officer did arrive, he also hung back. When a group that shares a common belief system, like police officers, hands over control to their commanding officer, they will often go along with the decision even if they feel it to be wrong—a failure of training resulting in a failure of muscle memory. Nationally, the plan since Columbine is that the very first officer on the scene pushes in to neutralize the threat rather than wait on backup officers.

Why didn't the principal use the public address system instead of the app, which is slow and can be problematic?

The PA system would have broadcast the threat instantly throughout the campus, while the app would require the recipients to be within reach of their phones and have their notifications enabled.

Why didn't officers engage the attacker through the exterior windows when they could not immediately get through the interior doors? Why was there a failure of command?

The answer to these last two questions must be an obvious lack of training and a failure to understand the priority of saving lives in an active killer situation. While courage can't be taught, the correct action can be trained, and that training will take over if the correct action is ingrained in the mind of the officer. Again, this is clearly an obvious failure to train and develop muscle memory. Failure of courage played also played a role. Some of those men and women who took an oath to protect and serve did not have the courage to put themselves in the line of fire.

This school, in this small Texas town of sixteen thousand people, was grossly unprepared for what happened that day, costing precious lives and putting a lot of people in danger. I will never understand why schools think it cannot happen to them. The parents, teachers, school administrators, and the school board members all watch television and see the news, and yet they don't prepare for an active threat/active killer event.

If you fail to prepare, you prepare to fail. But whom are you failing? Your children. Your teachers and staff. Your community.

The full seventy-six-page Robb Elementary Investigative Committee Report is easily available online, and I highly recommend that you read it, as it delves much deeper into the details of the incidents leading up to the attack and the timeline of events on May 24. You can also read more of my thoughts on the Uvalde massacre in an article published in *The Federalist* on June 10, 2022, entitled "The Uvalde School Shooting Was a Failure of Leadership, Not Gun Laws."

PART TWO:

What Does It Mean to
Have a Safe School?

When performing a school security assessment, I consider previous school attacks and try to get into the head of the attacker, just as I did in the opening scenario of this book. What would I do here to cause damage? How can I breach the perimeter or the gate(s) to get into the school and get close to students? "Think like the enemy" is a Red Team approach to testing security.

Many school attacks are similar to one another, starting with the initial breach of the perimeter, which could be a gate, fence, building door, or classroom doorway. Once inside, the active killer controls the environment from that second forward until he stops, takes his own life, or is neutralized by a good guy with a gun. The goal of school security is to see them coming. By that I mean *literally* see them breach a fence or a gate or know they are potentially coming because of reported observable concerning behavior.

A safe school is one that has a plan for any type of attack. It is a school where security has no political involvement or interference from boards or elected officials, where security is directed and managed by professionals in the field, not by "committees" of educators who think they know what to do. Often, I have told school administrators that I would have no idea how to select proper textbooks or develop a curriculum, and they should not think that they know how to properly secure a school without professional guidance. Yet, many try.

A safe school is one with very limited access. This means that it has very few entrances, or choke points, that are protected by armed and trained school security or police officers on or off regular duty. Authorized vehicles have current window stickers, and visitors must have an appointment and register before they enter.

A safe school is a zero-fail environment.

At a safe school, students might be required to have clear backpacks.

A safe school is one where the head of school believes and practices safe school protocol, where classroom doors are always locked during class without exception, where there is a practiced lockdown protocol. It's a place where lockdown is the default action to a bomb threat or even a fire alarm if flames or smoke are not seen or smelled.

A safe school is one where the principal, dean, or head of school is committed to making the school safe and will discuss that with parents openly and frankly. It's a place where security and safety are not driven by budget or an ad hoc "security committee," but guided by clearly identified security and life safety needs, implemented by a qualified head of security.

In safe schools, all staff have instant communication by portable radios that are always turned on.

A safe school is a school where all staff are continually trained and certified in stop the bleed, CPR, use of an AED (automated external defibrillator), and first aid, in that order. *All staff* means everyone from the gardener to the head of school. If I ask a teacher, a custodian, or the track coach who the first responder is in an active killer situation, their answer had better be, "I am."

A safe school generally has a camera room, commonly called

a security operations center (SOC) or command post, staffed by security professionals, where the school's cameras are monitored and recorded on motion at all times. In addition to monitoring all activity in buildings and surrounding property, today, CCTV video management systems can act as an alarm on motion and alert security if a fence line is breached, for example. This advance notice may allow time for a lockdown. Having a good video management system makes a huge difference in system capabilities.

A safe school has armed and trained security or current law enforcement officer(s) present at all times when children are present, before, after, or during school. A bad guy with a gun can only be stopped by a good guy with a gun.

A safe school is one that has a solid relationship with local law enforcement and notifies law enforcement of threats and criminal activity. It's a school that invites law enforcement to train in the school after hours and tour the school so that all officers know the layout of the building and the grounds.

The key word here is TRAINED.

Proper Training Is Key to Safety

On November 17, 2022, a Vermillion, Indiana, sheriff's deputy shot a high school student who was assisting him in a drill at the school. First news reports on the shooting stated that "an officer's gun fired on accident." According to the article in *American Military News*, "the incident was an accidental discharge of a firearm by a law enforcement officer."[11] In my opinion, this was a negligent discharge by the officer, who had to have

---

11 Willetts, Mitchell, "Student Shot During School Drill When Officer's Gun Accidentally Fires, Indiana Officials Say," November 19, 2022, https://americanmilitarynews.com/2022/11/student-shot-during-school-drill-when-officers-gun-accidentally-fires-indiana-officials-say/.

actually pulled the trigger in order for it to fire. Pistols are inanimate objects, and as such, they don't discharge on their own.

There is absolutely no reason on earth why the officer should have removed his duty pistol from his holster. There are plastic "blue guns" specifically designed for training. They are plastic replicas of real pistols or even rifles, and all departments should have them. Most departments and professionals teach Colonel Jeff Cooper's Four Rules of Gun Safety:

- All guns are always loaded.
- Never let the muzzle cover anything you are not willing to destroy.
- Keep your finger off the trigger until your sights are on the target.
- Be sure of your target and what is behind it.

What happened in Indiana gives all officers a bad name. The officer involved would have had to violate more than one of the above rules in order to shoot that student. If he had followed just one of the rules, the incident would not have occurred. That's why I say that training is important for all officers, whether they're PD, sheriff's department, or private security.

Assessment Checklist

Now that you have an idea of what a safe school looks like, do you think your school is safe? When I go into a school for an assessment, I use the following basic checklist of questions as a starting point. Read through the list and check off the questions you know to be true. This way, you're able to get an idea of where your school currently stands on its level of security. The following are considered minimal security/safety requirements:

❑ Does the school have a written lockdown plan for such events as active threats, active killers, bomb threats, trespassers on campus, and similar threats? If so, has your school drilled on the plan? The school should drill on the various types of emergencies to develop muscle memory on each individual's responsibility during the event. The first few drills should be done with staff only. Schools should also invite law enforcement so they can see the campus, meet employees, and give honest feedback about the process. At some point, it's important to involve children of an appropriate age to practice the drills with your staff.

❑ Is there a flip chart or simple reference guide in every classroom that covers lockdown procedures, strangers on campus, health and safety policies, fire drills, emergency procedures (such as 911 calls), tornadoes, severe weather, etc.?

❑ Does your school remind your community (parents, students, employees) to immediately report suspicious behavior to both the school and to local law enforcement? Are students asked to be aware of other students' activities on social media and to report concerns with guns, threats, videos of blowing up schools, etc.? All school attacks have had numerous red flags presented far prior to the attack. Reporting these red flags, along with early and appropriate intervention, is the first step to prevention.

❑ Has the school made clear that any threat or comment about shooting someone or bombing the school will be taken seriously, even if the comment was made in jest? Students should clearly understand that, just like at the airport, there is no room in the school for any type of comment, behavior, post, text, or possession of any type of threat.

❑ Does your school have appropriate policies that permit you to search bags, backpacks, computers, iPads, phones, vehicles, or any other personal items, and any place on school property?

❑ Has the school considered requiring clear backpacks so everyone can see the contents at a glance?

❑ Do classroom doors properly lock from the inside? Have you practiced and had timed locking drills? From the time you call a lockdown, do you know how long it takes for the full school to be locked down? Many schools start out with a three-minute process and, with practice drills, get the timing down to thirty seconds. It could save lives.

❑ Do you have a closed campus? Is it fenced (first layer of your layered security)?

❑ Are there limited entrances or gates as a second layer of security?

❑ Are the entrances/exits staffed by guards?

❑ Do buildings have limited and controlled points of entry and exit (choke points) as a third layer of security? Are other doors locked against entry from the outside? Any open door should be monitored by an actual person with a radio. You should not have the doors open or unlocked even for drop-off and pickup. It might inconvenience students and parents at the end of the day but may save lives.

❑ Are teachers and staff trained in stop the bleed, AED, CPR, and first aid? Are they currently certified in these techniques?

❑ Does the school have emergency response bags with at least twenty Soft T 1.5-inch tourniquets in each bag?

❑ Does the school have a supply of Narcan available?

If you don't know the answer to any of the questions here for sure, take the book or the checklist to school with you and ask. Take the list to a school board meeting. Get answers. Knowledge is power, and once you know, you can start pushing for the proper changes to make your child's school as safe as possible.

"But who is the best person to ask?" might be your next question. Do you know your school's organizational structure? Who's in charge of decision-making when it comes to safety and security? Who has the answers?

Let's find out.

School Leadership

You may be familiar with your school's principal and vice principal, the secretary, some of the teachers and coaches, and maybe you know a few people in the Parent-Teacher Organization (PTO). That's all fine and good, but do you know who actually *runs* your school? Who makes decisions about the budget and whether or not enough of it is being allocated to school safety and security? Who is in charge of the people who are in charge of your children?

The real question becomes: If the unthinkable happens, who owns it?

Who is personally, legally, morally, and ethically responsible for my child's security and safety at school? What is the name of that person and how do I contact them?

Think about this for just a moment: you send your child off to a place five days a week for eight hours a day. Your child or children are the most precious things in your life. Do you know who it is making the decisions that affect almost 50 percent of their waking lives Monday through Friday, and even more if they're involved in after-school activities?

Let's briefly outline the workings of a typical school district here, just so you get a basic idea. While the following is a sample structure, it's important to remember that not every school is structured exactly the same way. And in fact, private schools have a different structure that's more streamlined, with the head of school directly responsible for decisions that may fall on the school board in a public school system.

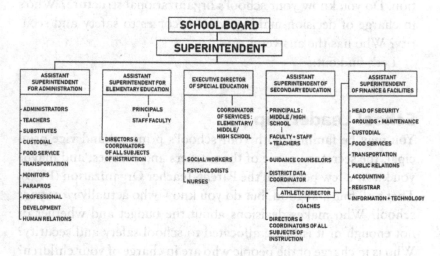

Take a moment to locate the school's director of security on that chart. Where do safety and security fall in the hierarchy of a typical school's organization? Who's in charge of hiring the director of security? It's important that the person in charge of hiring the person responsible for keeping your school safe knows the proper qualifications for such a position.

Ask your school administration for a chart of your school district's organization. Sometimes you can find this online on the school district's website. When you see that chart, take note if there is even a director of security box on it. Not a manager, not a contractor, especially not a committee, but who is the director of security?

Believe it or not, when I started looking up flow charts for the organizational structure of various school districts online, I found the director of security box missing on many of them. I suppose that could be an indicator about how seriously the school district takes the safety of the children in its charge.

It is important for you to know the organizational structure of your own school and then get to know the school officials and staff whose names fill those boxes. Do they think safety is important? Not just the head of security (if there even is one), but the official above him or her, and the one above that one? Do your school board members, and the president of your school board, hold the safety of your children in the highest regard? Does your superintendent? Are they showing that by allocating the appropriate funds to safety and security?

The job of the school board is to represent you, the citizens, on education and school-related issues. The school board members are elected officials who have a direct say in the operations of your schools, and they also are responsible for hiring and firing the superintendent. It's the board's job to listen to its constituents and to do its best to address the concerns of the community within the realm of education.

The organizational buck stops at your elected school board. Above them is YOU, the citizens of your community. You all vote for your school board at your municipal elections, so it's important that you get involved and understand where each candidate lands on crucial issues before you go to the ballot box.

School boards typically meet once a month, and it's important to remember that school board meetings are open meetings. Go to the meetings. Make your concerns known. Ask your questions, get involved, and keep doing it until you're satisfied with the level of security at your school. Then, keep an eye on it. Never give up. Just like the buildings and grounds need to be constantly maintained, so does the school security program.

If you're not quite ready to attend a board meeting, you can send a letter or email to your school board members or superintendent asking them to address your concerns. You can also do this preemptively if you plan to attend a meeting, so they can be prepared and so that some of your questions could possibly be answered prior to the meeting itself. Please feel free to use the following sample letter as a template, adjusting as needed to your specific concerns:

School Board/Superintendent Sample Letter
The following letter is easily adaptable to your superintendent's name, school name, and address, etc., or it can be modified to say "school board" instead of "superintendent."

Jane Doe
Superintendent of Neighborhood School
1234 Oak Street
Anywhere, Any State 12345

EMAIL/ Re: Life Safety/Security at (school name here)

Dear Superintendent Doe,

I am a concerned parent of a student at (school name), and I am writing to request general information regarding your plans to keep our students safe. As you know, school crimes including active shooters/active killers happen too frequently across the country. No school is immune from violent attacks.

Does the school district have a plan in place? Are the schools having lockdown drills? Is the school district working with local and state law enforcement on a regular basis to protect students? Are all teachers currently trained and certified in stop the bleed, CPR, AED, and first aid by the American Heart Association? Do our schools keep doors locked so that the school has

---

limited access? And finally, what is the security budget for this school year?

These questions can generally be answered by either a yes or no without divulging methods or techniques that may or may not be in place at (name of school). Thank you for your attention and I look forward to hearing from you soon.

Sincerely,

Your Name

Seems pretty simple, right? In theory, it should be easy to converse with your board members and superintendent, because you all have the same goal: to provide the best possible education for your children while keeping them safe at school. Sometimes it is that easy, and other times you get yourself up against a school board or superintendent that pushes back. In that case, you just have to keep pushing. Don't give up. Keep going to the board meetings and asking questions. Talk to the PTO and other parents. Talk to the head of security yourself if there is one. You are a stakeholder in your child's education. You care about your child more than anyone else. If you're not going to fight for their safety, who is?

Okay, now that you've done all this legwork, hopefully you've gotten some answers and you understand where your school stands on security. If the answers you were given are not satisfactory, or if you're still getting the runaround, it might come down to dollars and cents.

Where Is the Money Going?

Money talks louder than promises. If you find out where the money is going, you find out what's most important to your school's officials. A school district's budget is generally public information. You should be able to access it easily, and the budget should be discussed at a public board meeting prior to its approval.

If your school board refuses to show you the budget or discuss the budget with you in regard to your questions about security allocation, that's a red flag.

But here's the deal: if the office doesn't have a readily available copy of the budget for you to read (they should), it's just a quick Internet search away. Type "[your county] school district budget [current year]" into your search engine, and it should pull up the budget page of your county's school district's website as one of the first search results. Alternately, go straight to your county's .gov website and search for the current year's budget. You should be able to find all the information you need in order to get an idea of where the funds are being allocated.

Now that you know where the money is going, do you think enough is going toward school safety and security? Look back at that checklist. Are there essential safety measures missing that could be easily implemented, but aren't? Then maybe they aren't allocating enough money to security. For example, simple sixteen-channel radios can be purchased on Amazon for as little as $18 to $20 each. If you were to purchase one for each teacher and staff member, you're looking at a very small investment for a high return. It just doesn't make sense when money isn't allocated for safety.

One of the common responses I get when I ask a school board, superintendent, or head of school why they haven't hired a head of security, or more armed security officers, or implemented any one of the other important security measures, is "We just don't have the budget for it." This is not an acceptable answer. I have said it already and I'll say it again and again until the point is driven home:

Budget-driven security will always fail!

Your school administration cannot approach security measures with, "Well, here's what we can afford." They have to approach their school's safety and security plan by saying, "Here's what we need. Now, how are we going to find the money for it?"

I'd say more likely than not, there is money somewhere that would be better spent on security than its current allocation. How much money is currently allocated for teacher and faculty travel? How much is spent on educational technology (that may or may not be necessary)? Your child's safety should be the number one priority.

I like to ask of the board members, "What is a child's life worth in terms of dollars?" Then, watch their faces and wait for an answer.

Grants for School Security

If there truly is a budgetary issue with funding all of the safety tools you need to keep your school safe, there are still options. One of those options is to apply for a grant to cover some or all of the expenses. There are numerous grants available for this purpose, but often, they are not being utilized.

A quick Internet search can pull up a number of state-specific grants available for school security, including infrastructure and implementation. The following is a list of both national grants and some state-level grants for this purpose. The money is there; all it requires is someone who knows how, or is willing to learn how, and is ready to take the necessary steps to ask for it.

National Grants for School Security

In 2018, Congress passed the STOP School Violence Act, authorizing nearly $1 billion for the US Department of Justice School Safety Grants through 2028. This resulted in two different categories for grants:

1. Bureau of Justice Assistance: This grant is allocated for violence-prevention training and anonymous reporting technology. The process for these grants can be found on the BJA website at bja.ojp.gov under the tab "Funding & Awards."

2. COPS (Community Oriented Policing Services) School Violence Prevention Program (SVPP): This program was allocated $50 million in grant money, which is specifically for school security equipment and technology and related uses, which includes the following, as per the Security Industry Association's 2021 Guide to School Security Funding[12] :

   a. Equipment: entry control, intrusion alarm systems, screening equipment, security lighting

   b. Other technology: two-way radios, duress alarm systems, emergency alerts/communication systems, identification/visitor management, school facility mapping, bus tracking/route mapping, video surveillance technology

   c. Additional uses: salary/benefits for coordination personnel (nonsworn, civilian), supplies, travel/training, consultant services

---

12 2021 *Guide to School Security Funding*, School Security Industry Association, (2021). https://www.securityindustry.org/wp-content/uploads/2021/11/school-security-funding-2021.pdf

You can find information on this grant process at cops.usdoj.gov/ under the "Grants" tab.

In 2003, the US Department of Homeland Security created the DHS Homeland Security Grant Program. There are three programs under this umbrella, all of which are managed by each individual state's State Administrative Agency (SAA): Operation Stonegarden, the State Homeland Security Grant Program, and the Urban Areas Security Initiative.

Additionally, DHS offers grants through its Nonprofit Security Program, which thus far has been grossly underutilized by public schools but has been used regularly by private schools. This program is for updates to security for nonprofit organizations considered high risk for a terrorist attack, which is exactly what a school mass attack is—a terrorist attack.

Information about these grants can be found online at Fema. gov. Click on the "Grants" tab and then click on "Preparedness Grants." You'll find all the information you need on this site, including links to each state's SAA.

The US Department of Education has funded over $1 billion worth of grants since 2020 through two different grant programs: the Title IV Flexible Block Grant Program, which can be found online at t4pacenter.ed.gov; and the Elementary and Secondary School Relief (ESSER) Fund, which can be found at oese.ed.gov, by clicking on the "Programs" tab.

These are just a few of the national grant programs available to schools across the country. Additionally, a quick search for "security grants" will lead to a great deal more local and regional grants that may apply to your school's specific needs.

The PTO President Who Thinks They Know Security

For reasons that I will never understand, when some politicians get elected to a school board or made president of a PTO (parent-teacher organization), they sometimes get a rush of power and authority and instantly think they know everything there is to know about everything, including school security. We saw this in some states during COVID. It is like they have a crystal ball and that makes them all knowing and prescient. In reality, they may be just rolling the dice and experimenting with your child's safety and security.

Who should be in charge of school security?

The simple answer is the full-time school security director or law enforcement school resource officer (SRO) who is armed and present at the school at all times when students are present.

What would a qualified school security director look like? What are the proper qualifications? In my opinion, the best school security director is a recently retired law enforcement professional who is still motivated and wants to work. At the top of my list of candidates will always be a recently retired US Secret Service agent. After all, we think that our children are more important or at least just as important as the president of the United States, don't we? A Secret Service agent who has worked in the Presidential Protective Detail (PPD) has the training and experience in assessments, advance planning, defending venues and more, and they have the local law enforcement contacts and liaisons the school needs.

Another option would be a local police or sheriff's supervisor from a tactical unit like SWAT (Special Weapons And Tactics). They will have worked with the Secret Service on protection detail support. In a perfect world, this would also be a *parent* who meets the above qualifications and experience. And yes, the school security director should always be armed while at school.

Speaking of being armed, I often get asked my opinion on *teachers* with guns. My answer: 99 percent of the time, I advise against teachers carrying guns at school, concealed or open carry. It is a matter of focus in that security should be security full-time. A teacher with a gun may be known to students and others. So, instead of bringing a gun to school, two or more students or outsiders could potentially gang up and take the gun from the teacher. Also, if there is a gunfight inside a school classroom, all other plans have already failed, and you are down to that last 5 percent of survival chances.

Choosing a New School

Perhaps you are moving to a new city or are in the process of choosing a new public or private school for your children. That's an exciting and important decision for you and your family, and it's not one to be taken lightly. Use the checklists in this book as a jumping point for questions to ask your prospective school administration.

Many private and some public schools will give you a tour of their campus, explaining their security policies and procedures in detail. Don't skip that step! If they don't offer it, ask for it. While looking up statistics about incidents in schools can be helpful, the reporting is not always accurate. It's much better to visit the school, take a tour, and get a firsthand feel for the climate of security on campus. If the school has a Director of Security, take the time to meet with him or her to get your questions answered.

Local & State Government: Dillon's Rule vs. Home Rule

Local and state governments regulate education policy, including both funding and pedagogy for public schools. The public schools in this country can be either dependent or independent. Most schools in the US are independent, which means they are exclusively run by their school district. A smaller number of schools are dependent, meaning they are run by their municipality, town, city, or county, possibly alongside their state government.

States are further divided into two different classifications: Dillon's rule and home rule. If you live in a state governed by Dillon's rule, local authority is going to be more limited. The law was enacted in 1868 as a safeguard against corrupt municipal governments, giving them less power at the local level and more guidance from state authorities. States with home rule grant local government greater autonomy, and power at the state level is more limited when it comes to local affairs. The bottom line is that it could be easier for your local government to pass rules and regulations regarding school safety in a home rule state because they have greater autonomy than the local government in a Dillon's rule state.

It's hard to create a comprehensive list of states that operate under Dillon's rule versus home rule because that list is constantly shifting as more states repeal what they consider to be an archaic law or pass legislation that loosens the state grip on local authorities while still maintaining Dillon's rule as their overarching system. States like Vermont and Virginia have consistently maintained their Dillon's rule status, while Michigan was the first to repeal Dillon's rule to favor local authority. Then there are states like California, where charter cities are exempt from Dillon's rule, but home rule counties are still limited by it. Your best bet to find out if your state is run by Dillon's rule or home rule would simply be to google "Is [your state] governed by Dillon's rule?"

When it comes to making laws that govern the security of our schools, it's important to know where the buck stops in your state and then get involved in your local, state, and national elections. Education is power. The more you know, the better you'll be able to not only make your vote count, but to get your concerns to the people who can make things happen.

Regular Security Assessments: A Necessary Precaution

A professional security assessment or survey conducted by a fresh set of eyes can be, and often is, an epiphany for school leaders. Most private schools have an assessment done yearly, because there are a lot of moving parts that change regularly, like buildings, traffic patterns, size of student body, security officers, gates, cameras, etc. It's necessary to recheck to make sure those changes do not compromise the security of the school and the school grounds.

I recommend an annual assessment for all schools.

Some states, like Florida, require public schools to use the state's online tool to do their own assessment and report back to the Department of Education, which closely monitors progress, changes, and repairs. Other states do not have that requirement. The best way to find that information is to google your state and "school security assessments" or ask your school administration. Your school should be completing a security assessment at least every year.

The Security Assessment Process

First, it's crucial that you check the credentials of the company and/or the assessment agent before you hire them. Just because they have a nice website or have worked in the education field does

NOT qualify them to assess your school, train your staff, or work with your children on security issues. I recommend looking for a professional with prior law enforcement experience, primarily Secret Service, or any agency or person who had responsibility for detailed advanced inspections of facilities.

Once your head of school or legal adviser has interviewed and hired an assessment agent, the agent will meet at the school and ask a series of questions similar to the checklist I gave you in the previous chapters. These will be questions like,

- Do you have a single point of entry?
- Does every staff member have a walkie-talkie?
- Do your classroom doors stay locked during class time?
- What keeps you up at night?
- What weaknesses do you feel exist at your school?
- On a scale of one to ten, where do you think your school ranks on security now and where do you want it to be?

Next, you will have an on-site visit. Here's what happens during a professional security assessment, which I perform regularly for schools and other institutions across the nation:

The visit will likely take two days or more, depending on the size of the school and how well it has stayed up to compliance. The agent will check for all of the items on the previous checklist. He or she will speak with your security team, teachers, and staff, and perhaps even parents and students. Local neighborhood crime rates will also be a consideration.

When the agent has completed their on-site visit, they will write a draft of a confidential report highlighting the areas in compliance and the areas of concern where they will make recommendations on how best to remedy the shortcomings. The assessment agent will send the head of school or the security director the draft report and make themselves available to discuss it further. If there is an immediate and urgent safety issue, the agent will not wait for the report; they will notify the head or school or the head of security right away while on-site. Examples of that would be propped-open doors, holes in a fence, broken cameras, etc.

It's also important to note that there is a difference between using a private security assessment company and a public agency, such as the local sheriff's office: a private company's report can usually be kept confidential as a draft and is not public record. If you go through a local law enforcement agency, while they can often provide a relatively good assessment, it's important to remember that their report may be a matter of public record and could potentially be viewed by anyone. There is a possibility there of exposing your school's areas of weakness to a potential attacker, if they were to go and look for the report.

On the last day of the assessment, the agent might ask the faculty and staff to engage in a tabletop exercise. A tabletop exercise looks similar to the opening section of this book, where a simulated attack scenario is described and then discussed in order to highlight flaws in their incidence response planning. The intent of the tabletop exercise is to get hands-on training in order to better figure out how to respond to an active threat situation. These are typically really engaging, stressful, and eye-opening experiences for everyone involved.

After spending days at a school looking at everything from locks and alarms to cameras and communications, and after providing detailed prioritized findings and recommendations, some schools revert to what I call the *paralysis of analysis*. They pay for the expert assessment, then during the after-action briefing before I leave, they tell me they understand. They'll even tell me that the tabletop exercise on the last day opened their eyes to the fact that they had no real emergency response plan. Yet, some schools think they must form a "security committee" to decide what to do next. This committee will then likely take weeks or months to make decisions for the safety of the children. I will never understand this form of approach avoidance. What comes to mind immediately is "My God, if the parents only knew."

I once told a security committee, "If you all plan to practice security design, I might as well perform appendectomies on weekends in the parking lot." I have never been accused of holding back my thoughts when it comes to the lives of students.

Show me a school, any school, anywhere, with a "security committee" and no security director or full-time police officer making the decisions, and I will show you a school that is at high risk. Hence, one of the reasons for this book.

Knowledge is power.

Safe School Letter of Recognition

Every school in the United States now has the opportunity to be rewarded with a high-quality frameable letter of recognition through the National Sheriffs' Association (NSA) School Safety Recognition Initiative (SSRI) for their ongoing school safety efforts. An application consisting of questions from six categories to include risk and behavioral/emotional assessment measures, physical security, policy and procedures, and emergency preparedness, is made available via the NSA. The letter of national recognition is issued to those schools that, upon submission and review, have passed the requirements as set forth by the NSA School Safety and Security Committee.

Not only is the NSA SSRI program for schools so that they can be recognized for their positive school safety and security practices, but it's issued by the stakeholders in our school's safety with the expectation and the hope that all schools will take basic steps to create safe and secure spaces for their students. Who are these stakeholders? Members of the National Law Enforcement School Recognition Initiative Advisory Board include the National Sheriffs' Association, Federal Law Enforcement Officers Association (FLEOA), the International Association of Chiefs of Police (IACP), the Major County Sheriffs of America (MCSA), the National Association of School Resource Officers (NASRO), the National Association of Women Law Enforcement Executives (NAWLEE), and the National Organization of Black Law Enforcement Executives (NOBLE). These are the men and woman who have made a commitment to keeping us safe. But in order to help them do their jobs, it's important for schools to meet their basic expectations of safety and security.[13]

This letter of recognition, prominently displayed in the foyer of your school, reminds parents and children of the school's commitment to safety and security. You can see the requirements for the letter of recognition and apply online by going to the website at www.sheriffs.org, click on the "Programs and Initiatives" tab, then down to the "NSA School Safety Resource Site" tab. There you'll find information about the program and application.

By answering the questions posed in the application, your school will also be able to gauge where they're at in their own security protocols, training, staffing, etc. They can then use the program to increase their security to the appropriate qualifying level. During the writing of this book, I accepted a seat on the NSA School Safety

---

13 "NSA School Safety Recognition Initiative," National Sheriffs Association, accessed on December 7, 2022, https://www.sheriffs.org/schoolsafety/ssri.

and Security Committee, and I very much look forward to serving in this capacity.

Whether you're approaching the board for the first time regarding school security, or your school is already going through an assessment process, the important thing here is that you're constantly taking steps toward a safer and more secure school for your children and the people who are there to educate them. You're starting to develop and implement a plan and remember that the side with the best plan wins. A potential attacker will likely have a very well-thought-out plan, often orchestrating the details of the attacks for a long time prior to the event, like in the case of terrorists.

We need to be planning longer, harder, and in more detail than a potential attacker. That's how we keep our children safe and alive. There is no good reason not to plan to keep our children safe. None!

Attackers only need to be right once. We must be right every time.

PART THREE:

About Alyssa

Lori Alhadeff stood beside her murdered daughter, hands on her body, trying to warm her . . . trying to bring her back to life.

"I didn't know at the time why she was cold," she said.

Lori was at the morgue, and for the first time since it all started, she was able to see where her daughter was shot: in the hands while trying desperately to stop the attacker's bullets, along the top of her head, and straight through her heart. Fourteen-year-old Alyssa Alhadeff was shot eight times by the killer who attacked Marjory Stoneman Douglas High School in Parkland, Florida. The day after the tragic event, her mother was still in shock that her young, vibrant, beautiful daughter was gone from this earth forever.

Four years later, we sat across from each other at Parkland Bagel, where it was obvious from the many greetings and smiles and quick conversations that Lori is a well-known and well-loved member of her community. Over bagels and coffee, she told the story of the day her daughter was murdered with tears in her eyes. I knew many of the details of the terrible event, since I had been hired as an expert witness on the case, but this was different. Listening to Lori and watching the deep pain resurface after all these years, it was all I could do (biting my lip) to hold back tears. I will never forget the anguish that I saw on her face.

"I got a text message saying that shots were fired at Stoneman Douglas," she says, recounting the tragedy from the very start. "Kids were running and jumping the fence. In that moment in time, I had this overall sense of grief and loss that came over my body, because I just knew that something was wrong."

Lori frantically drove to the school. She parked her car on the sidewalk and started running. Groups of parents were gathered there along with law enforcement from various agencies.

"I was just trying to figure out, looking at Alyssa's schedule, where she was in the day." She wanted to find her daughter. Where was she on campus? Was she out of the line of danger? Then Alyssa's best friend came over to Lori in the crowd.

"Where's Alyssa?" Lori asked frantically.

"I don't know," Abby replied. Moments later, Abby received a text message from another friend: Alyssa had been shot.

"I immediately just fell to the ground and started screaming," Lori says. "In this fight-or-flight situation, your mind is just spinning. I was in fighting mode." She had to get to her daughter.

In Lori's mind, the thought that Alyssa had been shot meant EMS was taking care of her. She'd be rushed to the hospital and treated for her injuries. Lori started pushing her way to the school, but a police officer pushed her back.

"I was directed to this reunification center at the Marriott," she says. "Nothing was even set up yet." There was nobody in there, so she got the hotel staff to help her call hospitals. Then a Broward County Sheriff's Office officer approached her and started talking to her. She was frantic and screaming, but instead of de-escalating the situation, he yelled back at her with no empathy for her at all. "I'm telling him that my daughter's been shot," Lori says. "And he's not believing me."

Instead, he asked her, "Well, how do you know?" He was insulting and cold, and Lori just needed to get to her daughter as fast as possible. So, when a total stranger offered her a ride, she took it.

On the way to the hospital, Lori saw a mass of police cars and officers near the school, and she thought they might be able to get her there faster. She got out of the stranger's car and into an officer's patrol car. He was a massive guy, taking up all the space in the driver's seat beside her. There was total uncomfortable silence between them. When they arrived at the ER, they thought Alyssa might be Jane Doe in surgery, but it wasn't her. Lori was panicked and exhausted and still desperate to find her daughter. She reassessed it and knew in her heart that Alyssa was still at MSD.

The officer she was with was not from the area, so back in the patrol car, she directed him to the school. But that's not where he took her; he took her to the reunification center again, which was now swarming with people. Hundreds of panicking family members of missing students were at the Marriott, including Lori's husband and parents. It was a madhouse.

"We were the people who couldn't find someone," Lori recalls. "And they kept pushing us and pushing us, and we ended up in this big ballroom." They had pizza and water and snacks. "It was like they were just throwing us stuff, whatever they could find." Lori wrapped herself in a Red Cross blanket and waited, getting no answers at all. After hours like this, she went into the bathroom and just screamed and cried—melted down.

Finally, around two o'clock in the morning, an FBI agent pulled Lori and her husband into a private room. "Well, I can't talk in front of your wife," he said to Lori's husband.

No, that wasn't going to happen. "You say it," she demanded. She needed answers more than anything else.

The FBI agent told her that her daughter had been shot in the face and was unrecognizable. A mother's worst fear— her daughter was dead. But in the very darkest, most horrific moment of Lori's life, this FBI agent gave her information that ended up being a lie. Her beautiful girl was never shot in the face. Alyssa was not unrecognizable. She was shot eight times, including straight through the heart, but she was definitely not unrecognizable.

In the wee hours of dawn, just as the sun was starting to rise, Lori drove to the Everglades, where she felt she might get closest to God. "I wanted to ask him, why Alyssa?" she says, with tears welling in her eyes. The sky was washed in oranges and yellows when Lori made her way to her mother's house. "We're going to the medical examiner's office," she said. She didn't know why. She hadn't even thought about it, she just felt somehow that this was the next step.

"I went in there and I told them I wanted to see my daughter, Alyssa," Lori says. "But they told me I couldn't see her." Instead, they went in the back and came out with an eight-by-ten-inch glossy color photo of Alyssa's face. It was her daughter, very recognizable, and this was the moment she knew for certain that Alyssa was dead. "The FBI kept saying, 'We believe Alyssa is dead,'" Lori recalls. "That left room for hope." But now, that hope was gone.

The Alhadeff family is Jewish, which meant they had to quickly jump into funeral arrangements in order to bury their deceased the next day, in accordance with Jewish tradition. They had to go to the cemetery and pick out everything, including what they were going to say and what to do for the funeral. They were not expecting to have to bury their teenage daughter. How can you even begin to prepare for such a thing?

When they'd made all of the arrangements, they were finally able to go and see Alyssa. The thing about death is that it's so still and so cold. Lori stood over her daughter, and her instinct was to warm her, but she couldn't. She looked over her daughter's body and saw where the killer shot her: in the head, in the heart, in her hands, where she had put them up to try to block the bullets. Before she left her daughter, Lori took a pair of scissors and cut off Alyssa's long black hair.

"I didn't want the shooter to take everything from me," she says.

After the funeral arrangements were made, the Alhadeffs went to Pine Trails Park, where there was a makeshift vigil happening. A long line of reporters stood on the edge of the gathering, and Lori was angry. She'd seen something on the news, something where the president was talking about "thoughts and prayers," and it wasn't good enough. Thoughts and prayers wouldn't bring her daughter back. Thoughts and prayers wouldn't stop this from happening to another family, wouldn't prevent the ruthless murder of another teenager.

Lori marched up to the first reporter. "I have something to say," she demanded.

The reporter tossed her hair to the side and flippantly responded, "Well, I'm not on the air."

So, Lori just went down the line, reporter after reporter, until she got to the very end, where someone handed her a live microphone. Lori didn't know exactly what she was going to say. She was propelled by something inside her, perhaps something stemming from her grief, her anger, her pain. "I called out President Trump to take action, to do something," Lori says. Well, the nation listened, and Lori's interview went viral.

They had the funeral and sat shiva, and within two weeks of the massacre, Lori and her husband, Ilan, founded the nonprofit organization Make Our Schools Safe. "I couldn't have my daughter get shot and killed and just sit back and do nothing," she says. While she didn't necessarily have a plan, she knew she was on the right track. "We were very lucky to have some amazing people on our board," she says. "And one of them is a marketing person."

He told her that the organization needed to narrow its focus down to maybe two goals in order for it to be successful.

Those two things would become the Make Our Schools Safe Clubs, which encourage and guide students to take stock in their own safety; and Alyssa's Law, which mandates the installation of emergency panic buttons linked directly to law enforcement in every classroom. At the date of this publication, Alyssa's Law was introduced by House Representatives in numerous states, and the law has passed in New York, New Jersey, and Florida.

Lori didn't really know how to get laws passed, but she learned. She knew that when a tragedy strikes, elected officials are compelled to do something. So, when Alyssa's old friend from New Jersey contacted Lori and said there was a law they were trying to pass in the Alhadeffs' home state and they wanted to name it after Alyssa, Lori was immediately on board.

The Make Our Schools Safe Clubs are now being implemented in schools all over the country. These clubs provide the structure for students to come together twice a month in order to take ownership of their school's safety and give them a platform for their voice. They meet regularly with school officials and also participate in fund-raising activities to help schools in need of important security improvements.

You can find all the information about Alyssa's Law and the Make Our Schools Safe Clubs, plus learn how to get involved and stay up-to-date on the organization's activities at makeourschoolssafe.org. You can also follow them on Facebook, Instagram, Twitter, YouTube, and TikTok using the links on their website.

In addition to running the Make Our School Safe organization, Lori was elected to the Broward County school board. This also was not something she'd necessarily planned, but as she was emerging as a noticeable voice in school security activism, she was encouraged by community members to run for a seat. She did, and she won. Lori was a teacher and a coach, so she knew the ins and outs of the public education system well. As a former educator and as a parent, she knew what needed to be done.

Over the last five years, Lori has dedicated her life to the safety of our children and the security of our schools. She has been interviewed on countless news networks, podcasts, radio stations, and for documentaries, and while the youth of Parkland used their voices to push for stricter gun laws, Lori used and continues to use hers to drive home the importance of school security.

She talks to parents and community members all the time about reporting observable concerning behavior, and she often reports it herself when people are unwilling or unable to do it themselves. She has built a remarkable relationship with her local law enforcement, an important component of keeping our children and our communities safe. She is a recognizable and outspoken advocate for our children.

Even as we sat at our little table and talked, a news report came onto the television on the back wall of the bagel café: nine-year-old faces felony charges for allegedly bringing a gun to school.

"It keeps going," Lori says. But that's why she keeps fighting the good fight, all while keeping the memory of her daughter close to her heart.

"No matter how many times you've spoken about your child's death," she says—hundreds of times for Lori over the past five years—"the pain never goes away."

She walks by Building 12 at Marjory Stoneman, the building where her daughter died, every time she takes her son to soccer practice. But she says that talking about it, whether to reporters or in interviews or just with other parents, is therapeutic.

Lori left us with one final thought: "Your voice is your power."

It's time that you use it. Now, before it happens again. Before

it happens at your school, because after it happens is too late. . . .
You can't bring them back.

We pray that you will never have to endure what Lori and
other parents have experienced. Now is the time to change the
dynamic before it happens at your school. Get involved now.

PART FOUR:

Children Under Attack

Whether you choose to address it or ignore it, the fact is that our children are under attack. Every few days while I was writing this book, another news report popped up: more young people were threatened or killed. It's not stopping, so the level of your preparedness is the most important defense against losing more children.

As Lori said, your voice is your power. I'd like to add to that sentiment:

Knowledge is the foundation on which to build your voice.

As a security specialist charged with keeping people safe, it's part of my job to understand attackers and even to think like them when assessing for safety. These are precisely the same techniques I used to keep executives and officials safe. For a decade, I protected former United States Secretary of Defense Donald Rumsfeld. This is also the same knowledge that I used when leading a Red Team for DHS after the events of September 11. Some of these are the same basic methods used by the Secret Service to protect the president of the United States. I believe that your children are just as important as the president, don't you?

So, using the decades of knowledge that I've accumulated working in both the public and private sectors, let me explain to you the types of attack that a killer might use to penetrate a school and kill students. If you want to beat the attacker, you need to learn to think like them and plan to defeat them. Think like the enemy.

The Complex Coordinated Attack

My biggest worry is always a complex coordinated attack (CCA). A CCA is truly an act of terrorism—as are any mass attacks on people for any reason—but with a CCA, the event involves intricate planning coordinated with multiple people at multiple locations at the same time or one right after another. These kinds of attacks also use multiple methods of death and destruction simultaneously, including bombs, firearms, arson, vehicular attack, or other more unconventional weapon systems.

Columbine was perhaps a failed CCA. If you recall, there were improvised explosives planted that failed to activate. Had that occurred, thousands of students and faculty could have perished.

The September 11 attacks were complex coordinated attacks, for example. These four simultaneous attacks were carried out by nineteen terrorists from an Islamic extremist network called Al Qaeda. They hijacked four commercial planes, crashing two into the Twin Towers of the World Trade Center in New York City and a third into the Pentagon. The last hijacked plane was destined for the White House, but it was derailed by passengers who revolted, and it crash-landed in a field. September 11 was the most coordinated attack in US history, and it was also done with minimal assets. That CCA cost almost three thousand lives and started the worldwide war on terror.

In preparation for the attack, seventeen of the nineteen attackers took flying lessons at the Boca Raton, Florida, airport, and they were notably only focused on taking off and flying, not on landing. Things may have turned out differently had someone been paying attention.

The attack on September 11 is the most devastating complex coordinated attack ever on US soil, and it drastically changed this country's feelings on safety and security. Now, when you travel by air, you must go through a thorough Transportation Security Administration (TSA) security check at the airport: they check you for weapons of any sort, including items like hairspray, pocket knives, box cutters, and even baby formula or any kinds of liquids; you have to take off your shoes and jackets (if you don't have TSA Precheck clearance); and you must remove electronics and limit your carry-on items. People don't have a problem when they have to go through this long and often frustrating process to fly, but when mass attacks are happening over and over again at schools, very little changes. This makes no sense to me.

According to the National Center for Education Statistics[14], close to fifty million students were enrolled in public pre-K through twelfth grade schools in the fall of 2021, and close to 4.7 million attended private schools the previous year (the most recent data available). According to the Federal Aviation Administration, 2.9 million passengers fly on US airlines daily[15]. So, let's look at these numbers again:

Close to fifty-five million students attend schools every day in the USA. Fewer than three million passengers fly in the USA each day. Tell me again why there's tighter security at airports than at our nation's schools?

If the 2017 Las Vegas shooting had been a CCA, thousands could have died rather than the sixty that were killed and 413 injured by the gunfire from the attacker's thirty-second-floor suite

---

14 "Digest of Education Statistics," National Center for Education Statistics, accessed December 7th, 2022, https://nces.ed.gov/programs/digest/d22/tables/dt22_203.40.asp.

15 "Air Traffic By the Numbers," Federal Aviation Administration, accessed December 7th, 2022, https://www.faa.gov/air_traffic/by_the_numbers.

at the adjacent Mandalay Bay Resort and Casino. The number of injured leaped to over eight hundred when adding in those who were trampled or injured in the panic that ensued. This is currently the largest mass shooting by (allegedly) one person in US history, and it's truly a tragedy. However, if the incident had been a CCA like the attack on September 11 or even like the attempt on Columbine, it would have left a much greater wake of death and destruction.

The Active Threat

An active threat is anything that is happening now, in the present. A trespasser on campus, or a police chase close to the school are both active threats, for example. Of course, in the cases of Sandy Hook, Columbine, Parkland, and Uvalde that we discussed in detail in Part One of the book, as soon as the perpetrator walked onto school property with a firearm, it became an active threat/active killer situation. This should always trigger an immediate lockdown.

The original name "active shooter" is also being interchanged with "active killer" or "attacker" for the purposes of this book. Why? No longer is the mass murder of innocent people being carried out *only* by means of firearms. These killers are killing by any means. They have murdered their victims with all kinds of weapons, including knives, swords, explosives, firearms, and automobiles. Sometimes they target and kill indiscriminately. Other times they plan their attacks at familiar locations, murdering strangers, acquaintances, or both . . . all innocent victims. Some mass murderers begin their rampages by first murdering family members.

Designating an active shooter, active killer, or active attacker simply indicates that the situation is taking place and in progress in real time. This activity should trigger an urgent and immediate response from school personnel, security, and law enforcement.

Bomb Threats

A bomb threat is a communication that an explosive device has been or will be placed in or around the school or building with the intent to detonate and cause bodily harm or death. Most bomb threats are received by phone, and they are to be taken seriously until proven otherwise. If you are on the receiving end of a bomb threat, ask the following questions:

- What is your name and address?
- Did you plant the bomb? If not, how do you know a bomb was planted?
- What type of bomb is it, or what does it look like?
- Where is it planted?
- What will detonate the bomb?
- What time is the bomb scheduled to detonate?

Keep the caller on the phone as long as possible and stay calm. Even if the caller disconnects, keep the line open until the police arrive. Do not trip the fire alarm. Do NOT evacuate the building. Many schools with no real plan continue to evacuate on a phone bomb threat. If the threat is a "target workup" or "probe," the bad guys will see exactly what happens and where the students will be in the event that he or she decides to follow through on the threat—outside and unprotected.

My advice is always NOT to evacuate on a bomb threat. If a suspicious device is found, that is a different story. If the device is outside, it may still be safer to lock down. Call 911 and follow the advice of law enforcement.

At the time of this publication, no bomb has been found or detonated at any school in the US following a bomb threat. In the unlikely event of an improvised explosive device (IED), students are safer inside the school. And generally speaking, if no suspicious device is found, the local bomb squad will typically not respond and search the school. All bomb threats should be reported to law enforcement immediately, and the school should have a clear and simple plan on how to handle the threats and make reports to law enforcement.

I repeat, the bomb threat response plan should NOT include evacuation. Evacuation on a bomb threat could be a target workup to a CCA, and it is not an effective plan in this instance.

The Potential for Terrorism

Many of us watch or read the news, listen to it, or get it in our Twitter, Facebook, and Instagram feeds. We see the millions of people from countries all over the world attempting to cross our southwestern border illegally, and some of those people are not people we want on US soil. In the first ten months of 2022, the United States Border Patrol had already made 1.66 million arrests of illegal migrants at the Mexican border, 25 percent of which were the same migrants being expelled and attempting to cross again, some for a third time (all three attempts are counted individually).[16] And while these migrants are crossing over from Mexico, they are originally from a wide range of countries including Cuba, Syria, Nigeria, Lebanon, Iran, Venezuela, Honduras, Colombia, Haiti, and Nicaragua.

At the time of writing this book, the Department of Homeland Security reports that ninety-eight individuals on the Terrorist Screening Database (TSDS)—also known as the "watch list"—

---

16 Montoya-Galvez, Camilo, "The Facts Behind the High Number of Migrants Arriving at the Border Under Biden," CBS News, accessed December 7th, 2022, https://www.cbsnews.com/news/immigration-biden-us-mexico-border/.

were apprehended at the southwestern US border[17]. Of course, we do not know how many others actually got through undetected.

Because of this, and because of the threats that have been made against schools both secular and nonsecular, I worry about schools as potential terror targets now and in the future. We have been aware of a number of terror plots against US schools and places of worship that have been interrupted by the FBI and other agencies.

In 2016, a Florida resident inspired by ISIS attempted to bomb a Jewish school and synagogue. He was carrying an explosive device when he was stopped on his way to the building, and according to the criminal complaint, the attacker said, "It's a war, man, and it's like it's time to strike back here in America."[18] Anti-semitism drove him to attempt a potentially catastrophic act of terrorism against a school and synagogue on US soil.

Schools that have words in their names that may be seen to represent America and American values, like "patriots" "American," or "eagles," may be potential targets for terrorists with anti-American sentiment. Schools with these words anywhere in the name of the school or sports teams should be vigilant about protecting themselves against acts of terror. Also, schools with specifically religious names, including both Jewish and Christian schools, could be marking themselves as a target. If you are one of those schools, hopefully you are in a city with a Joint Terrorism Task Force (JTTF) organization, and they are watching intelligence and any terror-related chatter about your school's name.

A terrorist attack is typically a CCA. Terrorists plan and coordinate to inflict the most amount of damage possible, and they

---

17 "CPB Enforcement Statistics Fiscal Year 2023," US Customs and Border Protection, accessed December 7, 2022, https://www.cbp.gov/newsroom/stats/cbp-enforcement-statistics.

18 Complaint at 5, United States vs. James Gonzalo Medina, (U.S.D.C. Southern District of Florida 2016) (16-mj-02562-wct).

want the world to know exactly why they did it. That's why the JTTF exists. The JTTF are "groups of highly trained, locally based, passionately committed investigators, analysts, linguists, and other specialists from dozens of US law enforcement and intelligence agencies."[19] This allows agencies to easily share information and work together to prevent and respond to crises through intelligence gathering and strategizing. The JTTF is led by the FBI.

It's important to know that the JTTF is working diligently to protect our spaces from acts of terrorism, but it's also your responsibility to become an active stakeholder in your child's safety. Make sure that the proper safeguards are in place at your school, because these kinds of outside terrorists aren't going to be within the realm of your personal ability to observe their behavior. They typically aren't striking from within your community. They are an outside strike, so you will be counting on your layers of physical security for protection.

When and Where to Evacuate

Now that you know the various types of threats, it's important to think about what happens should one of those threats come to fruition. Especially when thinking about bombs or fire alarms going off, your first inclination might be to evacuate. Just get out of the building, and fast. But that's not always the answer.

Think before you evacuate: consider the exposure risks to students and staff.

It is perhaps instinctive to want to evacuate on a bomb threat, for example. But as I said in the last section, students are generally

---

19 "Joint Terrorist Task Force," US Department of Justice, accessed on December 7, 2022, https://www.justice.gov/usao-wdmo/joint-terrorism-task-force.

safer locked inside classrooms until law enforcement arrives and takes charge of the situation. The same is true for an actual fire alarm unless there is an obvious presence of smoke or flames.

In the case of an active shooter, or even a fire alarm or bomb threat, after the initial lockdown is over and the threat has been contained, first responders may begin to evacuate the buildings in an orderly fashion. Buildings should NOT be evacuated prior to these first responders' controlled initiation of their evacuation process.

Following are the appropriate responses to two nonshooter threats: fire alarms and bomb threats.

Fire Alarm Sounding—Not a Drill: It is recommended that your school NOT evacuate on an actual fire alarm unless you see fire or smell smoke. At times, students have pulled the alarm. In many school shootings, the active killer pulls the alarm to initiate a lockdown so that students are outside their locked classrooms. It has been over sixty years since a child died in a school fire in the United States. A fire alarm sounding that is not a required fire drill should initiate an immediate lockdown response. The announcement on radios, on any channel, would be, "Lockdown, lockdown, lockdown—this is not a drill, this is not a drill. Lockdown, lockdown, lockdown—this is not a drill."

Bomb Threat: I recommend that a bomb threat should initiate an immediate lockdown. Nine-one-one should be called from a different phone than the phone that received the threat, and the receiving phone should not be hung up even if the caller disconnects the call. Police will investigate the threat itself but normally will not search the school if there is no suspicious device found. Our research indicates that there has never been an actual bomb when a threat was called in. On the other hand, a called-in threat to cause an evacuation could be a target workup by an active killer, forcing students out in the open for easier access to those students. In the unlikely event that there is a bomb outside the school, evacuation would be forcing students into harm's way. In a few school attacks, the active killers placed improvised explosive devices in or near cars in the parking area. The announcement on radios, on any channel would be, "Lockdown, lockdown, lockdown—this is not a drill, this is not a drill. Lockdown, lockdown, lockdown—this is not a drill."

The lockdown involves locking all doors into the school. Classroom doors should be locked. If there is a window in the door, it should be blocked with curtain or Velcro on cardboard. Students should be move to a safe wall and asked to keep low, below two feet. Window blinds should be closed. Cell phones should be put on vibrate, and students should not talk aloud.

The desired outcome in any situation like this is to protect your children, yourself, and the staff of the school. SUSTAINED INTERVENTION EQUALS SURVIVAL. It's important that we all recognize our normalcy bias right now so that we can keep our schools safe for our children.

Layers of Security

The layered security approach works for schools, houses of worship, sporting events, etc. It works to protect the president and other public officials; I know because it was my job for many years to protect some high-profile people, and I believe your children are every bit as important and valuable.

On a school campus, usually there should be at least three layers, starting with the outside perimeter, which could be a natural barrier like a lake or a river, a fence with a main gate, or a constructed barrier. A second layer could be SROs or police officers patrolling between the outside perimeter and the school, in a designated parking area, etc. The final layer would be the locked school with locked classroom doors. The goal of layered security is to know that someone or something that doesn't belong is coming—an early warning system, if you will—and to prevent them or it from getting to our children.

Following is a checklist of ways to properly establish your school's three layers of security:

Outer Layer of Security: natural barriers or fencing at least six feet high; security cameras; single or minimal points of entry, locked and/or guarded.

Middle Layer of Security: a controlled gatehouse, SRO and/or police officer(s) staffing the gatehouse and patrolling the grounds, continuously monitored security cameras.

Inner Layer of Security: Limited points of entry into the school that are monitored, all staff with walkie-talkie radios. Ballistic film covering existing windows, locked exterior doors, locked interior doors (always locked during class time), hard rooms— safe rooms that have heavy or bullet-resistant doors.

The layers of security are a really solid foundation for building a safe school. As I mentioned previously, once an attacker gets all the way in, especially into a classroom, chances of mitigating loss of life is very low.

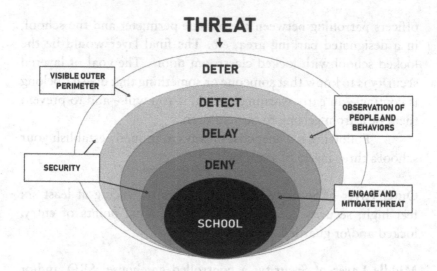

Deter, Detect, Delay, Deny

Here is a simple way to remember the layers of security:

Deter: Make it obvious to anyone contemplating an attack or collecting information for a potential attack that your children, your school, and its staff and families are a hard target. You could deter would-be attackers with the presence of a secure campus.

Detect: Detect and acknowledge all persons spending any time near your school grounds or your student body when they are outside the grounds (i.e., buses for field trips and games, etc.), regardless of whether or not they seem suspicious. Identify them while they are still outside or at a distance. Have a solid plan in place and practice situational awareness.

Delay: If the attacker moves past the first two phases, the goal would be to frustrate and ideally prevent their intrusion or attack attempts.

Deny: Finally, if the attacker makes it past all the previous phases and gets into the school, classrooms will be locked down. Deny the attacker the ability to harm anyone by utilizing the lockdown methods practiced in your school's lockdown drills.

Reunification as Part of the Plan

As you read in Lori Alhadeff's compelling story, the reunification center at Parkland was chaotic, at best. When there's an active attacker at a school, parents who are missing children are going to be frantic. Emotions will be running high, and it's the job of the first responders handling the reunification area to de-escalate and keep things running smoothly.

Reunification is a necessary part of any school's plan. It is a specific and safe location, typically a mile or two from the school, where parents and students can be reunited in the wake of an attack. The reunification location should be discussed with local law enforcement and first responders so that everyone is on the same page. This location and this plan should also be clearly and repeatedly communicated to the parents and families of the school. Like a lockdown drill, the repetition of the plan is the primary way to get it to stick, because most parents will instinctively race to the school and try to find their child. We have seen this over and over in many school shootings or emergencies.

In that communication, your school should make the reunification plan clear to both students and parents. The plan is to keep everyone as safe as possible, because if masses of parents race to a site where there is an active killer still at large, or possibly multiple attackers and/or explosives, they're not only putting themselves in harm's way, but they could also be encumbering law enforcement, preventing them from effectively doing their job.

PART FIVE:

Preventing an Attack

Y ou know the old adage "An ounce of prevention is worth a pound of cure." Preventing an attack is by far the better option than having to engage in an active killer situation. There's no real cure when lives have been taken. So, safe schools do everything they can to prevent an attack before it is active, starting with paying attention to and reporting observable concerning behavior.

Observable Concerning Behavior (OCB) & Situational Awareness

Observable Concerning Behavior

As you read in the terms section, observable concerning behaviors are like red flags for a potential school attack. Sometimes, these OCBs are stressors. For example, the attacker at Uvalde's mother had died just prior to the attacks. While he definitely had OCBs prior to that, the death of his mother could have given him that push. Other OCBs are things like social media posts depicting cruelty to animals, bullying behavior, being bullied, stating that they are going to commit acts of violence, or photos of themselves with weapons. OCBs can also be incidents at school such as fighting, being a victim of bullying, or being socially ostracized, and withdrawal from peers and/or family.

Attackers usually have multiple motives, and almost all school attackers had negative life factors including bullying, abuse, abandonment, or social isolation and other stress factors at some point in their lives. Their specific motivations for attacking a school can and do vary. Some attack the school because of a personal vendetta against particular people in the school or the institution itself. Others carry out their act of violence on schools because they're copycatting a previous school attack. In this case, they've studied these attacks and are motivated by the fame or the notoriety that the killers received as a result. These attackers want to be noticed.

One commonality between the majority of school attackers is that they begin planning and start to acquire gear, supplies, firearms, IEDs, ammunition, etc. These are not in-the-moment crimes of passion; they are meticulously planned and carefully executed acts. So, there are typically plenty of OCBs (red flags) along the way, such as photos or comments on social media or gun shop customers noticing that the attacker didn't seem stable.

The Video Game–Violence Connection

Another thread that runs between many school attackers is their use of violent video games. Colonel David Grossman, in his book *Assassination Generation: Video Games, Aggression, and the Psychology of Killing*, makes a solid argument that these video games can instigate school and other shootings by way of encouraging and normalizing aggressive behavior. I am not saying that use of first-person shooter and other violent video games will always instigate violence in their users. But I what I do assert is that when some other variables are present, violent gaming can lead to violent actions, or at the very least, violent gaming can be an outward indicator that the gamer is drawn toward death and violence.

If you notice someone who is particularly obsessed with violent video games, keep your eyes on them. Do they display any other characteristics of violence, depression, hatred toward a particular group of people, self-isolation, or self-harm? If so, it's important to report your concern to your school administration and/or the local PD.

OCB Checklist

Here is a brief checklist of observable behavior that could be concerning in regard to potential attack threat. This list does not encompass every OCB but gives you a good jumping point to understand the types of behaviors you should be looking for:

- Social media posts about:
  - Guns and ammunition
  - Weapons of any kind, including knives and bombs
  - Violence against schools or other people
  - Violence against animals
  - Animosity toward a specific religious, ethnic, or political group
  - Suicide or self-harm
- Obsession with violent video games
- Changes in behavior, including self-isolating, drastic drop in grades, personal hygiene habits, and withdrawing from previously enjoyed activities
- Drastic shifts in sleep patterns: insomnia, lack of sleep, or heavily oversleeping

- Drug or alcohol use
- Verbal or written threats
- Brutality toward animals
- Physical altercations including with friends, family, or strangers

If you see or hear of any combination of these behaviors behaviors and they have you feeling uncomfortable, it's crucial that you report them immediately and to all possible agencies. This includes:

- Nine-one-one if you believe the behavior requires immediate intervention
- Local law enforcement agencies, including local PD and sheriff's office
- School administration/school's head of security
- Child Protective Services (if the person is a youth)
- Federal and state law enforcement

The US Department of Homeland Security has implemented the If You See Something, Say Something initiative, which focuses on raising public awareness of the signs of terrorism and concerning behavior. If you go to their website at dhs.gov/see-something-say-something, you can click on the "Report Suspicious Behavior" tab, then click on your state for a phone number where you can report OCBs and tips directly to your state and local agencies tasked with preventing attacks. However, in all states, if you see an *immediate* threat, the best course is to pick up the phone and dial 911.

Reporting Apps

Some schools and communities use a reporting app for parents, students, and community members to report suspicious or concerning behaviors anonymously through their cell phone or computer. If your school offers an app, make sure you have it downloaded and know how to use it before you need it. It's also important to remember that it's crucial and potentially life-saving for dangerous behaviors to be reported immediately to law enforcement and school administration.

Once You've Reported the OCB, What Happens Next?

Your school should have a policy in place to deal with observable concerning behavior, and that policy should be made clear to parents and staff members at the start of every school year. If your school does not have such policies, or does not clearly communicate them, then you might have a safety and security issue. This includes not only behavior that's been reported but also behavior that's been observed directly by the school staff and students while on school property. When a school does not have a clear policy in place, things can go very wrong very quickly. Policy provides a clear pathway to resolution.

Mental Health Intervention

Some of the most secure schools in this nation have at least one full-time employee who, as part of their job duties, scans online activity for OCBs and student mental health issues daily. Their counseling staff is on high alert and ready to intervene with any appropriate means, including therapy and counseling for troubled youth.

This particular school also has a student task force that anonymously monitors social media sites like TikTok, Instagram, Facebook, and Twitter for any mention of violence, weapons, threats, school shootings, etc. This is something you can encourage your child to do as well or you can do yourself as a parent. I'm not saying you should stalk your child's classmates, but it doesn't hurt to keep an eye open when you're surfing for cute puppy videos on TikTok. PLUS, it is important to be a bit of a watchdog on your own children's social media. An involved parent is the best intervention for their own child or for children close to the family.

When a situation of bullying or other disturbing behavior is reported it's important that a team of experts is brought in to evaluate the situation, not just one administrator or social worker. This team could include a school psychologist, a social worker, a CPS agent, one of the student's teachers, the director of security, and a local law enforcement agent.

A real focus on mental health of the students and faculty in the community is a crucial part of keeping everyone safe. It is so much safer and healthier to get help for someone before it turns into a tragedy than it is to have to react when someone reaches the point where they are trying to cause harm.

Situational Awareness

Situational awareness, quite simply, is just the act of knowing what's going on around you. When you develop your situational awareness, you can take in a lot of information about your surroundings and quickly make an assessment based on what's there.

Let's pretend you're in a restaurant eating dinner with your family. Two men walk in together and, without greeting the maître d', they start walking toward the middle of the dining area. Do you notice them? Do you see how their bodies are moving? Are their eyes steady or shifting? What are they wearing? Are they in classy, fitted suits? Or maybe they're wearing loose jackets with their hands in their pockets?

If you pay any attention to the men at all, will normalcy bias prevent you from taking a closer look? According to security expert Steve Tarani, normalcy bias is a way of self-soothing: you think, *It's probably fine*, and then you can go on with your meal in relative comfort. But normalcy bias will also prevent you from taking action that could save your life or the lives around you.

I'm not asking you to live in a state of perpetual fear and anxiety. Quite the opposite. If you work on developing your situational awareness, you'll actually be able to relax knowing that if something is out of the ordinary, you'll catch it and know how to react accordingly.

When we are thinking in terms of school safety and a potential attacker coming onto campus, take a look at the following chart of characteristics that could be red flags:

SIGNS OF A POTENTIAL ATTACKER

Inappropriate or ill-fitting clothing	Illegal parking or unnecessarily parking close to an entrance
Hiding hands in pockets, jacket, or bag	Unfamiliar with surroundings
Continuously touching something that is concealed (likely a weapon)	Agitation
Strange lumps in clothing, especially near the midriff, belly, small of the back	Irritation, visible frustration
Continuously touching clothing	Intense focus in one direction
Constantly checking or keeping eyes on an item on their person	Constant prayer or repetition of one phrase, often quietly
Clothing that seems way too big or baggy	Mumbling
Leaning on or favoring their dominant side	Indecisiveness
Protecting a potential weapon with their body	Communication issues
	Pacing or coming and going multiple times

Would you see it if someone was exhibiting small behaviors like this? Have you noticed behavior like this in the past and ignored it? It could be nothing, but it would be better that you notice and it ends up being nothing than if you do nothing and it ends up deadly. So, how do you notice?

First, whenever you're in a given situation, take a moment to look around. Does everything seem normal for the type of area that you're in? Second, use your senses: sight, sound, touch, smell . . . maybe not taste. Sometimes one thing will be off and that will be the tip that something's wrong. Maybe it's the faint smell of gasoline or the sound of a person very quietly mumbling repeatedly under their breath. Don't assume something is okay when it seems off. You have to trust your gut.

Finally, stop the tunnel vision. All too often people get so overly absorbed in the video on their phone or the article they're reading that something could be happening right in front of them and they don't even realize it. Just like I'd say not to go jogging with music blaring in your headphones, I'm telling you not to get sucked into your phone or a book or even too much into a conversation to the point where you don't notice your surroundings.

Situational awareness is very much about being present in the moment, in your space. I know it's getting more and more difficult with all the distracting gadgets that vie for our attention all the time, but it's possible with a little bit of honing. The more you practice, the more honed you'll get. It's simple and free and one of the most effective tools in your arsenal for preventing attacks.

If you want to learn more about how to effectively develop your situational awareness, read Steve Tarani's compelling book, *Your Most Powerful Weapon: Using Your Mind to Stay Safe*. I highly recommend it.

The Outer Perimeter

If observing and reporting concerning behavior does not thwart the attack before it ever has a chance to develop, it's now up to your outer perimeter to stop the attacker from gaining access to the school.

A school campus should be no different than a gated community, a limited-access apartment building or condominium complex, or your own home: it should only allow entry onto the property to those who belong or have a legitimate reason to be there. This means that your school should have a closed campus.

There should be a limited number of points of entry onto the school property, and those should be gated and/or guarded at all times. If your school does not have a fully fenced perimeter with limited access points, you have a school security issue. In the case of Parkland, the attacker drove right up in front of the school in a ride-share car. He should not have been able to do that. The property should have been gated, only allowing access through window sticker, pass, key code, or call box: or each entry should have been guarded by armed security.

If you want the very best option, the school will have one primary entry point that remains available throughout the day. This entry point will have a guardhouse, the IDs of all guests will be scanned, and the trained guard will ask a series of questions before giving them a guest pass sticker, which includes their name and photo.

At one such school, there was an instance where a guest did not prominently display his guest pass, and it landed him in a bit of a situation! This school is particularly good at security; they make it a part of their culture from the time the children enter preschool. On this particular day, a man was visiting the school, but he put his pass on the upper thigh of his pants, then his jacket happened to fall over top of it. Well, he happened to also be wearing all black that day, and when he went into a bathroom, a five-year-old kindergartner saw him: a stranger, dressed in all black, with no guest pass! The child immediately notified his teacher, and when the man came out of the bathroom just moments later, there were two armed guards waiting for him! This is an example of good security at a school that makes it a priority.

So, your school's outer perimeter should be fully fenced with limited guarded and/or gated access points. The fence should also be five feet or higher, and if possible, it should be monitored by cameras and/or patrolled regularly.

Bollards, Door Locks, and Bullet-Resistant Glass

If an attacker were somehow to make it past your perimeter, then you're relying on a secure area directly around the school and a building that's locked tight to keep your children safe. We are now past the point of prevention; we are relying on a secure school building and its surrounding walkways and motorways to keep an attacker out—or at least slow him down.

Bollards: Protection Against Vehicle Attacks

I know when we think about a school attack, the first thing we often think about is a gun. But one of the most dangerous weapons is a vehicle, and an even bigger problem is that sometimes a vehicle-related occurrence is *accidental*. I always say that the most dangerous person on campus is a parent on a cell phone in the pickup or drop-off line. Nine people are killed in the US every day by distracted drivers.[20] A vehicle is a powerful, massive weapon that not only has caused accidental death but has also

---

20 "Distracted Drivers," Centers for Disease Control and Prevention," accessed December 7, 2022, https://www.cdc.gov/transportationsafety/Distracted_Driving/index.html.

been used intentionally to attack groups of people gathered in outdoor public spaces.

How many vehicles go in and out of your school grounds each and every day? How close can they get to your children? Do children stand behind a barrier of any kind until vehicles picking them up come to a stop? Are parents instructed to put cars in park and stay off cell phones while on school grounds?

Properly placed bollards are your best protection against a vehicular threat, whether planned or unintentional. Bollards are sturdy, short posts that block a vehicle from moving through a specific area. You may notice bollards or large planters at federal buildings and courthouses, for example. Some bollards are removable, and others are permanent fixtures. I recommend bollards along the pedestrian area at the pickup and drop-off line, as well as in any high-trafficked outdoor space at the school to which vehicles may have access. Note bollards or large planters at federal buildings and courthouses, for examples.

Door Locks: A Simple Defense

Door locks are such a simple solution, but one that's often overlooked or intentionally ignored. Why? Maybe because it's "easier" to keep the doors open, or perhaps a lock is broken and it's taking a while to get around to fixing it. But when we know unequivocally that locked doors prevent death in the case of an active threat, there are no good excuses. Had the doors been locked at Parkland and Uvalde, they could have mitigated the damage done in those schools. Those children didn't have to die.

Show me a school where some of the doors don't lock, and I will show you negligent administration.

The exterior doors of a school should ALWAYS remain locked, with access only to be gained at limited entry points that are monitored by armed SROs or police officers. Interior doors should always be locked during class time, no exceptions. No exterior door or interior door should ever be propped open. Locked doors save lives.

In addition to the regular door locks, schools could install doorstops on doors that are similar to the steel flip latches on the interior of hotel room doors. These stoppers either attach to the doorjamb or floor and can be easily accessed and locked quickly in case of emergency. Many schools in this country use a brand of doorstop called Nightlock. At Robb Elementary School in Uvalde, where a broken door lock allowed the attacker into a classroom where he killed innocent children, an inexpensive steel doorstop would have saved lives.

It's important to keep in mind that an attacker is going to look for unlocked doors. Even if he has to go down the hallway and keep trying, every door he attempts to open buys crucial seconds that could save lives.

Bullet-Resistant Glass or Ballistic Film: Creating a Fortress

Just like a home invader or thief, when an attacker can't get through a door, his next option is to shoot out or break a window. But what if your entire school building was an impenetrable fortress that most bullets could not get through nor hard objects could shatter?

Bullet-resistant window film placed on window glass is capable of turning rooms into a type of fortress. This type of product provides a similar protection to standard bulletproof glass at a fraction of the cost . . . and it works! I personally tested one particular brand of bullet-resistant window film, and it stopped bullets fired at close range. The balloon on the other side of the glass coated in ballistic film didn't even move. It is remarkable. In fact, I visited a school here in this country that used a bullet-resistant film from American Defense Structures to turn an entirely glass lunchroom into a safe room on campus.

Fully Trained Staff

Your school's staff members, including maintenance, grounds-keepers, teachers, assistants, coaches, administrators, and cafeteria staff, all must all be trained alike, because this training provides another layer of protection for your children. They should all have the listed first aid training and situational awareness briefings, and they should all be on radios and know how to use them properly. It should be made clear that they are stakeholders in their own safety and the security of the children under their charge (in loco parentis) and they are literally the first responders in an active attack situation. If the staff members are properly trained, there's a much higher chance that they will take the proper action if and when the time comes. If they're not trained or properly briefed on security issues, do not assume they will take any action at all.

Would you be more or less likely to jump into a dangerous situation if you didn't know what to do? I'm guessing the answer is "less likely." Now, what if you knew exactly what to do and had practiced it many times? You see what I'm saying, right? A football team doesn't take the field without first having learned and practiced the plays. Then once they're on the field, their muscle memory takes over. Our kids' safety is at least as important as a football game, isn't it?

A fully trained, fully invested staff member will know the importance of making sure doors are locked and never propping them open. A fully trained, fully invested staff member will not let someone into the building who hasn't been approved, and they'll know where the staged tourniquets are located and how to use them. They'll know how to properly lock down in an emergency situation. They'll know whom to call when they encounter observable concerning behavior. They will keep their walkie-talkies on and charged. They will not prop open exterior doors, and they will keep classroom doors locked. They will report OCBs and do their best to intervene.

Is your school's staff adequately trained in Stop the Bleed, CPR, AED, and first aid in that order of importance?

Your head of school needs to take the lead on this. If he or she believes that the safety and security of your children and their staff is a high priority, so will the teachers and other employees. The teachers that I've spoken with over the years are grateful when the administration prioritizes safety and security and are typically eager to participate in any programs that help accomplish the goal of a safe school. The plan for security is zero fail.

Important Tools for Safety

I strongly recommend some important tools that will help teachers and staff most effectively protect your children. Once these tools are implemented, they will become a natural part of the routine and an important part of their jobs.

Walkie-Talkie (Radio) Communication

Radios are the most efficient and effective way to instantly communicate simultaneously with the entire school when there is a safety situation or a security breach. Whenever a staff member has a radio, the call goes out instantly to everyone who needs to hear it. Plus, if you have an off-duty police officer on security staff, that call can immediately go from an internal communication out to the entire police department with one click from that officer's police radio.

In active killer situations, seconds count.

When your child is on the playground or in the drop-off or pickup line, do the playground attendants or outdoor staff have walkie-talkies? Not cell phones, but walkie-talkies? There should be instant communication between any staff member on the outside of the hard perimeter of the building (school walls) and the staff inside. There are very good walkie-talkies that reach up to one mile and cost an average of $17 each. Budget should not be a factor.

Walkie-talkies should be kept in classrooms when class is in session, and teachers should keep them on their person when they leave their classrooms. At the end of the day, walkie-talkies can simply be left on the charging port in the classroom so they're ready for the next morning. For office staff, the walkie-talkies can be left in the office or classrooms to charge. This will become routine for staff members very quickly, and it's the most effective tool for on-campus communication.

Walkie-talkies are also the best off-campus communication when it comes to activities outside the school, including bus transportation for drop-off and pickup as well as for field trips and sporting events. Bus drivers and field trip chaperones should have instant radio contact with the school security office at all times.

Security Cameras

It doesn't do any good to have security cameras if no one is watching them. Nor does it do any good if those cameras are on a delay or not properly serviced, as we saw in Parkland, where officers, due to a video delay, continued to report the attacker was on the third floor when he had already vacated the building. This is not helpful at all. In fact, it's a hindrance. So, a fully operational camera room or Security Operations Center is vital to the school's safety, and cameras must be monitored, in real time, by a specifically trained security person at all times when students are present.

Ideally, cameras should be placed on every outside wall of the building, and cameras mounted flat with a 180-degree range are much better than a corner-mounted camera because they give you a broader and clearer field of vision. Generally, we recommended that cameras be mounted on outside walls at approximately eight feet off the ground, well under tree canopies. Inside cameras should be mounted on walls so that they are recording faces, not just images of people moving. Too often camera companies decide to locate cameras on ceilings because it is an easier installation for them. Cameras should also be placed in all interior hallways of the school as well as high-trafficked areas like cafeterias and foyers. The Security Operations Center should look like NASA by the time all the cameras are up on monitors. There should be nowhere for someone who is unknown to the school to move from point A to point B without being spotted by the SOC personnel monitoring the cameras.

First Aid Essentials That Save Lives

The following tools are not just recommended—it's my opinion that they should be required in every school in this country. Every classroom and office should have a first aid kit and several good tourniquets…and every nurse's office should have Narcan stocked and know how to use it. The first aid kit is obvious and is something you'll find in every nurse's office, but the tourniquets are something that a lot of schools miss. A few "jump and run" bags stationed around a school, depending on the school's size, should have at least twenty 1.5-inch Soft T tourniquets in each.

In the Parkland attack, there were students who may have bled out from their injuries before the first response medical teams got to them. Timely and properly applied tourniquets are a crucial part of saving lives from excessive bleeding. Every classroom should have staged tourniquets (which means they are ready to use and not in the original plastic bags), and every teacher should be trained in how to use them. I'd say, to take it a step further, middle and high school students could also be trained in how to use a tourniquet. Many schools train older students on stop the bleed, CPR and first aid.

Narcan contains the active drug naloxone, which is an opioid antagonist. If someone overdoses on an opioid, like heroin or fentanyl, Narcan is your first and best defense to save their life. So, this should just be in high schools, right? Wrong. Especially in light of the fentanyl "Skittles" epidemic, Narcan should be stocked at all schools, including elementary schools. These fentanyl "candies" are deadly and should be watched as a potential tool for a terror threat on school children.

"According to the CDC, 107,375 people in the United States died of drug overdoses and drug poisonings in the 12-month period ending in January 2022" is a statistic quoted from the DEA website. "A staggering 67 percent of those deaths involved synthetic opioids like fentanyl."[21] The new way that the fentanyl is being packaged, pressed into colorful pills that resemble popular candies like Skittles and SweeTARTS, makes it the perfect product for drug dealers to market to our young people across the country...and that's just what they're doing. According to the DEA administrator Anne Milgram, most of the people who overdosed on fentanyl didn't even know they were ingesting the deadly drug until it was too late.[22]

There was a sharp increase in fentanyl overdose at schools in 2022, ranging from seventh-grade boys all the way to seniors in high school. Just two milligrams of fentanyl is enough to be fatal, especially for someone who has not built up a tolerance to opioids. These are kids getting the drug on false pretenses or being given the drug by the perpetrator with the intent to cause harm.

---

21 "Fentanyl Awareness," United States Drug Enforcement Administration, accessed on December 7, 2022, https://www.dea.gov/fentanylawareness.
22 Ibid.

In 2022, over 50.6 million doses of fentanyl-laced fake prescription pills along with over 10,000 pounds of powdered fentanyl were seized by the DEA, with a large portion of that coming from the Mexican drug cartel.[23] This drug can be as deadly as a bullet, and yet one of the school superintendents where students accidentally overdosed on the drug reported that the district did not stock Narcan at its schools,[24] an antidote that saves lives every single day.

Targeted naloxone distribution is the CDC's number one evidence-based strategy for preventing opioid overdose[25].

Narcan or other brands of naloxone are free through your state and local health departments and through many nonprofit organizations. The Narcan emergency kit can include a nasal spray and/or an auto-injector device plus instructions on how to use them. Video instructions are also readily available on the Internet.

There is no reason not to stock Narcan in every school's health center, and absolutely no reason for the staff not to know how to use it.

Alert Apps

As a backup to the instant notification via walkie-talkies, there are apps available to schools that are made specifically for reporting red flags (observable concerning behavior) anonymously. This

---

23 "Drug Enforcement Administration Announces the Seizure of Over 379 million Deadly Doses of Fentanyl in 2022," Drug Enforcement Administration, accessed April 25, 2023, https://www.dea.gov/press-releases/2022/12/20/drug-enforcement-administration-announces-seizure-over-379-million-deadly.

24 Crane, Emily, "Boy, 13, in 'Grave Condition' After Fentanyl Overdose at Conn. School," *New York Post*, (January 14, 2022), https://nypost.com/2022/01/14/teen-overdoses-on-fentanyl-at-hartford-connecticut-school/.

25 "Evidence Based Strategies for Preventing Opioid Overdose: What's Working in the United States," Centers for Disease Control and Prevention, accessed December 7, 2022, https://www.cdc.gov/drugoverdose/featured-topics/evidence-based-strategies.html.

type of anonymous reporting is vital primarily because students often fear retribution if they "tattle" on someone, or perhaps they don't want to report something and risk embarrassment if it turns out to be nothing.

The apps can be used to report a behavior they've noticed from another student, and they can also be used to instantly report a real-time issue such as a fight breaking out or a student carrying a weapon. These apps are good if properly used as a matter of solid policy, and in addition to instant communication via walkie-talkie.

When looking into your school's use of alert and reporting apps, ask these questions:

1. Are there police officers as well as admins on the apps?

2. Does the app report to a central emergency call center which then notifies law enforcement, or does the app have a direct line to the police station?

3. What is the school's process for dealing with an anonymous report that comes to them via the app?

In many states, schools are required to report suspicions of abuse, but schools should also have a plan to report to law enforcement any incident of a student, teacher, or staff member bringing a weapon of any kind onto school property. Law enforcement involvement is the key to successful use of the app, and ultimately to success in creating a safe school environment.

Panic Buttons

Panic buttons installed in every office can be an inexpensive option for schools looking to back up their walkie-talkie systems. Hardwired or wireless panic buttons can often be installed by the school's existing burglar alarm company, or they can be purchased as their own system from various companies and ring only internally.

The intent of the panic button is to provide a quick alert via a central alarm monitoring station to local law enforcement in the case of any kind of emergency, including an active killer situation. The alert goes to a central security office, where a staff member then immediately calls local police. Panic buttons can be installed under a desk, behind the reception desk, and at other convenient locations. They can also be portable or worn around a staff member's neck on a lanyard.

Alyssa's Law, as discussed in Part Three, is a law that would require schools to install panic buttons in every classroom. To see if your state has instated Alyssa's Law, you can check online at makeourschoolssafe.org. Even if the law has not been instated, you can ask if your school has panic buttons and request that they install them if they do not. Panic buttons are an inexpensive safety measure and a good tool to have as another layer of security.

Automated External Defibrillator (AED)

Currently, there are very few states in the US that have laws on the books requiring schools to have an AED on-site, and this needs to change. But until it does, it's your job to advocate for the presence of this lifesaving device in your child's school.

Mounted in easily accessible parts of the school, the AEDs could provide much-needed seconds when someone is suffering from sudden cardiac arrest. Did you know that sudden cardiac arrest is the leading cause of death among young athletes?[26] And it can occur after intense periods of physical activity. So, why not have a potentially lifesaving device that only costs around $1,500 on-site and ready?

26 "Sudden Cardiac Arrest," Children's Hospital of Philadelphia, accessed on December 7, 2022, https://www.chop.edu/conditions-diseases/sudden-cardiac-arrest.

...rest is the leading cause of death annually, compromising, and it can occur after sudden ... or physical activity. So why not have a potentially life-saving device that only costs around $1,500 on-site and ready?

PART SIX:

The Role of Security Officers and Law Enforcement

Your school security officers and local law enforcement officers are your primary defense against a potentially fatal attack on your school. These officers should be armed and highly trained in order to provide the best possible deterrent and defense from a threat of any kind.

First of all, for an attacker, seeing armed security guards and police officers around the perimeter fencing or gate(s) can be an instant deterrent. They don't want to get caught or shot before they can get into the school and make their point. Also, the presence of officers shows the potential attacker that the school takes security very seriously. *If they have adequate officers, then they must prioritize security and have other measures in place.* So, when the attacker sees guards or officers, they may not even try.

Second, well-trained officers are aware of their surroundings, and they should act swiftly and effectively when a situation arises. The officers are also trained in firearms and practice regularly for accuracy. Remember, the best defense against a bad guy with a gun is a good guy with a gun—a good guy who knows how to use it.

Third, if you have one off-duty police officer on campus, you have dozens of officers waiting as backup with any request for assistance call from his or her radio. A police officer carries both the school walkie-talkie and their police radio with them at all times, even when they're working off duty. That radio call goes instantly to the entire local police department. In this case, you get a lot more than what you pay for.

The clear presence of police or armed security officers on your campus, and the indication of a strong relationship between the school and local law enforcement, sends a message that you take the safety and security of your school seriously. A school without an SRO or police officer present at all times is a soft target.

But don't police officers on campus make kids feel nervous or unsafe? Hogwash!

While there are administrators and parents who think that kids feel unsafe with police officers on campus, I feel it's important for the next generations to grow up building a trusting relationship with the police officers who are paid to serve their communities. When your director of security interviews the potential candidates for his or her team, they will do so carefully, because not only are they choosing the best person to protect the students, but their choice will also form these young people's opinions about our men and women in uniform.

In most of the schools that focus on security, the students have an excellent relationship with the armed officers on campus. The officers are often invited to eat lunch on campus with the students, so they build a bond of trust and confidence. These men and women become a part of the community they are committed to protect. Many are parents. Many have children in school. They are an integral line of defense that cannot be overlooked.

Armed vs. Unarmed Security on Campus

There is a truism in security: the only thing that stops a bad guy with a gun is a good guy with a gun. If a school decides (usually for financial reasons) to have *unarmed* security only, that administration is making a huge mistake that could cost the lives of your children, in my professional opinion.

Unarmed security is an oxymoron. A "security guard" without a gun is really only a greeting or concierge service. They end up giving directions and helping kids find their lost headphones. They're not real security. In fact, for a serious attacker with a plan, unarmed security can be provocative. Unarmed officers will rarely stand between a gunman and your child.

Now, as I said before, a good guy with a gun needs to know how to use it. Both police officers and officers employed by a hired security firm will have some degree of firearms training. In most states, a uniformed police officer is required to attend a firearms range and qualify once per year, unless they're in a specialized unit like SWAT. Many private armed security officers, depending on the company, qualify quarterly and are often more accurate shots than their law enforcement counterparts. If the attacker gets through the outer layer of security, and especially if he breaches the building itself, you absolutely need that armed officer to mitigate the damage or even still prevent any damage from happening at all . . . because remember, if the attacker gets close enough to hurt someone, and officers have to draw their guns, the layered security plan has failed and the students and staff are in the last 5 percent of the survival matrix.

Building a Relationship With Law Enforcement

It's important that the schools build a good relationship with their local law enforcement, even if the school does not employ off-duty police officers as part of their security force. This is because, after the school staff and the school resource officers, the local police department may be the next line of defense against an attack . . . and one of the most important partners in addressing OCBs. Your local PD can be part of the prevention, not just the intervention. To the community at large, the police get called whenever there's a concern of any magnitude, especially when it comes to anything potentially threatening. You want the PD to have an open line of communication with the school so that if they become aware of OCB from one of the students enrolled, your school faculty knows about it, too. Early identification means a higher chance of heading off potential violence before it begins. That's the best-case scenario. Remember, the school is in the education business—not the threat-investigation business. This is a law enforcement function.

Here are some questions to ask your school leadership about their school's relationship with law enforcement:

- Do your local chief of police and sheriff's offices have copies of the school's blueprints and a map of the campus?

- Does your local PD know your plan in case of an active killer or threat?

- Does your school administration work with the local first responders on a reunification plan?

- Do SWAT and other special units train at your school (when there are no classes in session)?

- Does your school have a clear line of communication with local PD in cases of observable concerning behavior?

It's important to your school's safety and security that you have a good working relationship with your local, state, and federal law enforcement agencies, as well as first responders like fire department and EMTs. When it's done well, the report of OCBs to one agency will quickly be communicated with the other. You should be able to report an OCB to the police and your head of school and expect that the two agencies will work together to address the issue. Communication is key in keeping a school and a community safe.

Does your school invite the local SWAT team to train at their school during days that school is not in session?

It is crucial that the officers who are highly skilled in disarming or neutralizing an active killer, the SWAT team, have firsthand knowledge of the layout of your school and they've practiced navigating your school's hallways and perimeter. In short, the SWAT team and other officers should be training at your school. The information and muscle memory the officers gain in these kinds of trainings could save deadly seconds in an active killer situation.

Finally, when your school engages in activities and opens the dialogue with the local PD and sheriff's office, the positive presence of the officers in their community builds the children's trust in law enforcement. They become not just people with badges and guns on the news, but real people, parents who care about the safety of human beings a great deal. Children who grow up with uniformed officers in their daily lives, greeting them, watching out for them, going to bat for them, will very likely develop a trusting relationship with and respect for their men and women in uniform.

PART SEVEN:

The Attack Scenario Revisited

L et's return to the frightening scenario that I presented to you on the first pages of this book. I will mark each paragraph with a number which represents how many crucial errors were made in that paragraph. After the paragraph, there will be lines corresponding with the numbers. Underline the errors in the sentence and then write down what should have been done differently on the lines. This will help you learn how to pinpoint the very spots where the attack could have been stopped, and how.

Tabletop Exercise

[3 ERRORS & 1 OCB] I walk in through the open gate at the back of the football practice field and make my way to one of the rear doors of the main building, which is propped open with a brick. I know how to get in. I've been here before. I went to school here! Teachers and some of the students will remember me. I sure hope they remember me because I sure remember them—the ones that picked on me and made fun of me. I hate them and I will shoot them. This will be a day they will NEVER FORGET! I will be famous for what I do today.

1. _____

_____

2. _____

_____

3. _____

_____

OCB: _____

_____

[1 ERROR & 1 OCB] The TV news will show my photo and talk about me for weeks—this is what I want—I want to show them. This will be just like the video game I used to practice with—NO ONE CAN STOP ME NOW (I am a punisher).

1. _____

_____

OCB: _____

_____

[2 ERRORS & 1 OCB] I will use the stairwell because there are no cameras there. Then I will unzip my duffel bag—really my rifle bag. I will use my father's gun. I also have 300 bullets of ammo. When the lunch bell rings the hall will be full of students—they are my TARGETS. My planning for this has taken weeks and I know it will work—they will be SORRY. I am soooo ready!

1. _____

_____

2. _____

_____

OCB: _____

_____

[1 ERROR – 2 POTENTIAL ERRORS] I told my best friend to stay home today. I told him what I will do—he promised not to tell on me. The bell will ring, and I will hear my targets coming—I will keep shooting as many as I can—I want to set the record for the most kills in a school! I am unstoppable! If classroom doors are not locked—I will go there next—like the movie *Killing Fields*—They will be sorry. Doing it—yea!

1. _____

_____

2. _____

_____

3. _____

_____

As you can see in this written tabletop scenario, there are so many places the attack could have been prevented. The sad thing is that this scenario was crafted from reality, based on information gathered from previous school attacks.

Tabletop Exercise Answers

Don't worry, this is not a fully right- or wrong-answer exercise. It's an opportunity to put into practice the things that you've learned. The following are my suggestions on how an error could have been prevented or an OCB noticed and reported that could have stopped this attacker from ever coming into the school.

The opportunity to prevent this attack begins long before the attacker walks onto school property. It starts when someone in the community, online or in person, observes concerning behavior: In this case, let's say he was obsessed with violent video games, he has a history of fistfights and milder threats, he was living with his father who has been threatening to throw him out, and he posted on social media about self-harm. His grades slipped from Bs to Ds and Fs over the last year of high school, and his personal hygiene suffered as well as his sleep.

These are all observable concerning behaviors that should have been reported and followed up on with some serious mental health interventions well before he ever planned the attack.

Tabletop Exercise

[3 ERRORS & 1 OCB] I walk in through the **open gate** at the back of the football practice field and make my way to one of the rear doors of the main building, which is **propped open** with a brick. I know how to get in. I've been here before. I went to school here! Teachers and some of the students will remember me. I sure hope they remember me because I sure remember them—the **ones that picked on me** and made fun of me. I hate them and I will shoot them. This will be a day they will NEVER FORGET! I will be famous for what I do today.

1. The gate should not have been open. It should have been locked or guarded with a constantly monitored security camera at the entrance point.

2. The back door should have been locked.

3. There should have been armed police or security present.

OCB: He had a history of being bullied that could have been watched and reported.

[1 ERROR & 1 OCB] The **TV news will show my photo and talk about me** for weeks—this is what I want—I want to show them. This will be just like the **video game** I used to practice with—NO ONE CAN STOP ME NOW (I am a punisher).

1. The attacker likely praised school attacks in the past. Also, news media needs to stop publicizing the names of these attackers.

OCB: The attacker was playing violent video games.

[2 ERRORS & 1 OCB] I will use the stairwell because **there are no cameras there.** Then I will unzip my duffel bag— really my rifle bag. I will use **my father's gun.** I also have 300 bullets of ammo. When the lunch bell rings the hall will be full of students—they are my TARGETS. **My planning for this has taken weeks** and I know it will work—they will be SORRY. I am soooo ready!

1. Cameras should be located in all highly trafficked areas and must be monitored at all times.

2. If his father had been more involved in his life, or some member of his family or community had paid closer attention to his mental health, they would have locked up guns and kept weapons from him.

OCB: Weeks of planning typically leaves some trace of observable behaviors: purchasing guns and ammo, posting on social media, spending large sums of money, online purchases, agitation, or extended periods spent alone, etc.

[1 ERROR – 2 POTENTIAL ERRORS] I told my best friend to stay home today. I told him what I will do—**he promised not to tell on me.** The bell will ring, and I will hear my targets coming—I will keep shooting as many as I can—I want to set the record for the most kills in a school! I am unstoppable! If classroom doors are not locked—I will go there next—like the movie *Killing Fields*—They will be sorry. Doing it—yea!

1. Even if the friend would have refused to make the promise, that could have caused the attacker to rethink his plan. The friend should immediately report the conversation to the police and the school administration.

2. POTENTIAL: If the doors are not locked, many lives will be lost.

3. POTENTIAL: If an alarm is not instantly activated, or an instant PA announcement or walkie-talkie communication does not occur, this could be a fatal error.

CONCLUSION

I t is 100 percent certain that another school attack will happen in the United States. That is the sad but honest truth. It is time for parents and older students to hold stock in their own safety. It is time for you to understand the gravity of the security decisions that are being made for your school and your children. The last thing you want is to be on the other side of an attack and say, "I wish I would have . . . " "We never thought it would happen here," and "We didn't have a plan." Families and loved ones who have endured one of these tragedies will never fully recover. They will never be the same again.

Hopefully, this book will help you understand the right questions to ask and the appropriate steps to take to be prepared, and even to cut off a potential attack before it happens. Make sure you are prepared. Make sure your child's school is prepared. Don't take no for an answer. Get involved. You could be saving lives . . . the lives of your children, who deserve nothing less than your full commitment to their safety.

Never give up!

AUTHOR BIO

Wayne Black has more than forty-five years of professional security experience in both the public and private sectors. He is the founder and president of Wayne Black & Associates, Inc. For more than a decade, Mr. Black was the security Adviser/PSD lead for former Secretary of Defense Donald H. Rumsfeld and the Rumsfeld Foundation.

Mr. Black routinely travels the country providing threat assessments and training for schools and houses of worship. He has personally supervised protection details and special threat assignments in the United States, Central Asia, the Middle East, Africa, Europe, and South America. As a contractor for the Department of Homeland Security after the events of September 11, Mr. Black supervised a classified "Red Team" conducting threat assessments at designated national security locations and events. Mr. Black has been qualified to testify as an expert witness regarding security in US federal and state courts. He is also a certified firearms instructor in pistol, rifle, and shotgun. Mr. Black served as a law enforcement group supervisor for the Miami-Dade State Attorney's Public Corruption/Organized Crime Unit. Prior, he was assigned to the United States Justice Department's Inter-Agency Task Force at the US Drug Enforcement Administration, where he received numerous awards and commendations from the Department of Justice and the United States attorney general. Mr. Black is a member of the National Sheriffs' Association's School Safety and Security Committee.

ACKNOWLEDGMENTS

I want to thank Melinda Bryce for her many hours of writing assistance and counseling at all hours, including nights and weekends, organizing this book. Melinda traveled with me to visit schools in order to really understand school safety and security firsthand. I could not have done it without her dedication to the project.

I'd also like to thank Steve Tarani of Certified Safe Schools LLC and the National Sheriffs' Association's School Safety and Security Committee for contributing their knowledge and confirming many of the recommended practices in the book. Melynda Lamb, a former schoolteacher, gave me great insight from a teacher's perspective, and US Army Delta Sergeant Major (retired) Kyle Lamb was a great sounding board regarding tactics against active killers. All encouraged me to write this book and continue to support me in my mission to secure our country's schools.

Lori Alhadeff was kind enough to recount the horrific hours and days immediately following the MSD Parkland shooting. Her heart-wrenching narrative helped us better understand the pain that parents who have lost their children to school violence endure, and her continued work to keep schools safe is invaluable.

I want to especially thank noted forensic psychologist Harley Stock, PhD, for allowing me to work with him on workplace violence and serious stalking cases for three decades. Last, but by no means least, I want to thank Jarred Weisfeld, who shared his own experiences and worked hard to make this project happen for the safety of our children.

PUBLISHER'S NOTE

I initially approached Wayne Black about writing this book because I noticed a lack of security in schools as well as a lack of information on the subject available to parents. There was nothing like this book on the market, and since parents are their children's most important advocates, I saw an urgent need. During the course of the project, an incident occurred in my children's school that opened my eyes even wider—every child deserves to be safe at school. Wayne has been integral in helping me understand and navigate the situation with my local school district, and I want to personally thank him for dedicating his life to keeping our children safe. I also want to thank him for becoming both a mentor and a friend.

—Jarred Weisfeld